D1291427

Suffer Little Children

An Autobiography of a Foster Child

Suffer Little Children

An Autobiography of a Foster Child

Dereck O'Brien

Breakwater
100 Water Street
P.O. Box 2188
St. John's, Newfoundland
A1C 6E6

*The Publisher gratefully acknowledges the financial support of The
Canada Council, which has helped make this publication possible.*

*The Publisher acknowledges the financial support of the Cultural
Affairs Division of the Department of Municipal and Provincial
Affairs, Government of Newfoundland and Labrador, which has made
this publication possible.*

*Cover concept by Gerald Squires. Photography by Mannie Buchheit.
The crucifix depicted is a memento of the author's childhood (Chapter
4).*

Canadian Cataloguing in Publication Data

O'Brien, Dereck, 1959-
    Suffer little children
    ISBN 1-55081-032-4

1. O'Brien, Dereck, 1959-   2. Abused children --
Newfoundland -- St. John's -- Biography.   I. Title.
V746.S18027   1991   362.7'6'092   C91-097552-3

Dedication

This book is dedicated with love and thanks to my wife,
Dale,
and our beautiful daughters,
Sabrina and Brittany.
And to Ronnie and Roy,
who lived it with me.

Author's Acknowledgments

I would like express my gratitude to the following people for their support:

John and Helen Decker, two of the warmest, and most understanding individuals I have ever had the pleasure to know; Terry Kennedy and family, for a friendship that rises above the past; Fred Horne and Weldon (Buck) Orser for uncovering the facts and helping me to understand what happened so long ago; David Day and Clay Powell for their relentless work and countless hours spent putting the pieces together and trying to make sense of a system that had gone wrong; Margie Linehan, Patricia Deveaux, Virginia Connors and Colleen Power for helping me through the whole ordeal of the Inquiry, and appreciating what I was going through—to you, a very warm thank you. Special thanks also to my editor at Breakwater, Kyran Pittman, for all her help and understanding. And to all the staff and my co-workers at the Newfoundland School for the Deaf, thank you for your cards, gifts and hugs—they meant so much. You are all very special people, and from the bottom of my heart, I thank you.

D. O.B

Foreword

*T*he year 1989 throbs in our hearts and memories like a deep wound that is slow to heal.

The first pangs were felt in late 1988, when it was revealed that several members of Newfoundland's Roman Catholic clergy had been sexually abusing children. Reactions varied; a few were cynical, more were outraged and some, disbelieving. After the first wave of accusations, it was still possible to hear some say, "I don't believe it. Someone's just trying to cause trouble."

If anyone espoused that sentiment in 1989, it wasn't expressed publicly. The new year brought a torrent of new allegations, too overwhelming for shocked sensibilities to absorb or staunch. Of these, the most horrific was the revelation that the highly regarded Mount Cashel Orphanage, run in St. John's by a Catholic lay order, had been the scene of sexual and physical violence for years—inflicted upon the children by their caretakers, the Irish

Christian Brothers. Minds reeled. How had it happened?

Responding to the demand for an answer, the newly elected Liberal government commissioned a Royal Inquiry, to be presided over by Mr. Justice Samuel Hughes. When televised public hearings began in St. John's in September, the testimony quickly yielded a new question: how had the abuse been *allowed* to happen? Bureaucrats, teachers and citizens, it seemed, had all aided and abetted the accused. Reports had been lost, pleas for help had been ignored, and heads had been turned.

Whenever the Inquiry became entangled in a Gordian knot of politics, the testimony of the victims cut abruptly through to the heart of the matter: the human cost. One of the most memorable and moving testimonies was that of Dereck O' Brien. As Dereck spoke, viewers saw the wounded child come forward to tell his story, eclipsing the adult who had been holding him back for so many years. It gave the public firsthand insight into the painful catharsisis through which victims of abuse must pass in order to survive. And it demonstrated—in real terms, not abstractions—the agony that the abuse had caused.

What amends will be made to Dereck and the other victims remains to be seen. At the time of this printing, Hughes' findings have not yet been released. Meanwhile, the healing—and the suffering—continues for the victims, the accused and ourselves as we await justice.

Editor

Introduction

I first met Dereck O'Brien, as did so many others, on television. I saw a husky young man testify about time spent inside Mount Cashel Orphanage, time spent in foster homes, time spent as a little child, huddled in the dark on a staircase, feeling frightened and alone in the world. He touched a chord in all of us.

I arranged to meet him, in that fall of 1989, because I was just starting research for a film, and I was looking for help and guidance, for a sense and a feel of what those early years were like.

That first visit set the pattern for many subsequent visits: an invitation for supper, time spent with Dereck, his wife Dale and the kids in the kitchen, getting to know a young family. Then, after dinner and dishes and kids to bed, we went down to the TV room he had built in the basement and plunged into his sharply-edged recollections of times past.

I brought a tape recorder, and I remember starting by asking Dereck what he could recall of the first time he saw Mount Cashel. He talked about being in a car with his little brother, seeing the imposing structure as they moved up the driveway, going in through the front door, what it looked like, who met them, where he went, where his brother went. As he went on, it was as though a film were running through his head. The detail of his recall was astonishing. Names, colours, the geography of rooms, where the radiators were, the lights, furniture, beds, desks—it came pouring out. How people spoke, how they looked, how they moved, and always, what he felt. The tape recorder turned and the hours passed as a world was vividly re-created in front of me.

At the end of that first evening, I suggested to Dereck that he write down any other things he remembered in preparation for our next session. When I arrived a few days later, Dereck had almost filled the first of what would become many black notebooks. Each time we met, he wrote more. Soon, the recording stopped, and I would come over just to sit and talk and to read more, for the writing kept on and on. Dereck went back beyond Mount Cashel, back to his earliest memories, to even more traumatic times. He recalled being taken out of his home, and his placement in a series of foster homes. The memories that poured out of him were so personal, so immediate and alive, I was often moved to tears.

The period when Dereck was writing what turned out to be the bulk of this book was not easy, either for himself or his family. I remember one evening, Dale telling me that often her nightgown was soaked, as the memories overwhelmed Dereck and the tears flowed as he clung to her in the night. It worried me, and it worried Dale, but the floodgates had opened, and nothing could close them. Now, many months later, she feels that the writing has helped Dereck, and that he is more confident and at ease with himself. A brave man, a brave family.

And so a book was born, out of pain and suffering, and the strength of a man who has proved to himself that survival has been attained. Dereck has written this book partly for himself to recover his own past, and as a way of stating who he is. It is also a book written for the benefit of others, for those whose own pain can be helped a little by Dereck's memories, and for all those who feel that a story such as this one is a cry for all of us to find ways of helping our society be more caring and careful of its children.

John N. Smith
March, 1991

"Are you Dereck John O'Brien?"
"I am."
"And were you born on October 2nd, 1959?"
"I was."

Hughes Inquiry, September 26, 1989

02 October 1959 to 28 July 1964

Resided at St. John's with both parents....

> from *Summary of Adolescent Care of O'Brien, John Dereck*

One

I remember living in a green house on Casey Street in St. John's with my parents, grandfather and two brothers, Ronnie and Roy. I don't have many memories. I can't remember seeing my mother's face many times—few images of her back then remain in my mind. She was gone for long periods of time, and we kids were left on our own, as my father spent most of his time in jail for petty crimes. My grandfather, who only had one leg, wasn't much help to us, because he was drunk all the time. The floor of his room was littered with urine and rum bottles that toppled over when I opened the door.

I have very few memories of my father living there, but I do remember he sometimes gave me money, which I would put into a sock in my bedroom drawer. Then, one day, he came into the house, went to my room and stole all my money. He said he was just going to borrow a few dollars and return it, but he never did. I cried because my daddy had taken all my money.

I was aware at a very young age that all was not right at home. During the day, no one was home to prepare meals. Night came, and still, my brothers and I were alone. I spent hours on end outside at night, without anyone telling me it was time to come in. I don't remember ever washing my face or hands, so I must have looked very dirty. I slept with my clothes on and never changed them. I guess I never knew I had to keep clean, because no one ever taught me the difference. Being dirty was just another part of life for me.

I begged people for money and went into stores asking for food. No one ever questioned it. One day, I went to the Salvation Army to ask for something to eat and was given an apple juice can filled with fish and brewis. I remember taking the foil cover off and smelling it. To this day, I remember how sweet and warm it smelled. I brought it home and shared it with my brothers. Another time, I remember begging at a house in the neighbourhood, where a lady gave me two slices of bread with jam. Begging was just a part of life for me.

I was always hungry, cold and dirty. The house we lived in was very small—more like a bed-sitting room, really—and the only source of heat was a stove. It was dark and run-down, and the rooms were always damp. I was afraid to go to the bathroom—at least, I think there was a bathroom. I remember a dark room that I never wanted to enter, so I would go into a corner and relieve myself on the floor. I don't recall anyone ever cleaning it up.

There was a small window in the kitchen that looked out on Casey Street. The glass was broken and covered with a piece of cardboard. Someone had given me a beagle puppy and while I was holding it, it jumped from my arms, through the window and out into the street. In a matter of seconds, my dog ran into the path of a car and was killed. I couldn't believe what had happened and I've never forgotten that moment.

I have since discovered that Ronnie had a twin brother. Aunt Barb, my father's younger sister, told me that when she came to visit, the baby's sleepers would always be covered with sour milk and he would need to be changed. My mother would let him stay dirty. My aunt said he was mentally handicapped and his mouth couldn't form suction, so he often went hungry. He died at the age of nine months. I've received reports that he had several rat bites on his face and neck when he died. No one was arrested or questioned in relation to this.

My mother was very young and hadn't had a very good life with either my father or her own parents. She said that when she was younger, her mother was very cruel and unloving towards her. My mother said when she worked at a fish packing plant, my grandmother took all of her pay from her. She didn't even leave her enough money to take the bus to work, so she had to walk.

She told me how she bundled us up one winter's day and took us to her mother's to ask for help. I had no winter boots, and Roy, the baby, was just wrapped in a blanket. She said I was always smiling and that day, walking in the cold in ankle-deep snow with only my white baby boots on, I was still smiling. She told her mother that we were cold and hungry, that she had no money to buy coal for the stove and no milk for the children. Her mother replied, "You made your own bed, now you lie in it," and shut the door in her face.

My mother said that she married my father only because she wanted to get away from my grandmother. Life didn't get any better for her after the marriage. She told me that he often beat her when he came home after a drinking spree. He would be gone for days at a time and didn't even bring home enough money for fuel or food, even though he must have been making fairly good money working for the city council as a labourer. I was told he spent a lot of time with his friends, drinking everything from aftershave to melted record albums. Eventually, his drinking cost him his job, and he wound up in jail for break and entry or something like that.

After serving his time, he went to Toronto to work. He began sending money to us, but it was spent in the nightclubs and taverns downtown where my mother usually spent her evenings. Many times, I woke up at night, crying for her. I'd see a light on in the kitchen and would go in, expecting to find my mother there to comfort me. I remember screaming and being very frightened when I discovered I was all alone. I would crawl back into bed and cuddle into Ronnie.

When she was home, she usually had a strange man with her and would send me back to bed. I suppose she was getting her first taste of freedom, and it got easier for her to go away and not worry about us.

Occasionally, she must have had some extra pocket money because we sometimes had a baby-sitter—a young girl who often brought along a girl-friend. I remember the sitter placing me on the bed one day, pulling down my shorts and underwear and fondling my private area. She then took her own clothes off and placed my penis between her legs, while her friend undressed and put her private parts over my face. I was very confused and didn't understand what was happening. For years, I thought that sexual abuse was when a man raped a woman or molested a child. I never considered myself a victim—not until that forgotten experience was retrieved from the closet of bad memories that I thought was closed forever.

On another occasion, the babysitter was cooking eggs when the frying pan caught on fire. I can remember seeing the house fill up with smoke, and hearing someone say that the house was on fire. I went out into the street and watched the firemen rush inside. Again, my mother was nowhere to be found. I doubt if she knows to this day that there was a fire.

Some time later, when my mother was on another of her outings, my father paid a surprise visit. My mother, who had dyed her black hair blonde, was coming up the street with someone when he saw her. He grabbed her, brought her into the house and began cutting off her hair when he found out where the money he was sending her had been going.

They soon parted ways for good, and we were once again left alone. This time, someone reported us to the welfare department. My Aunt Barb, who was eighteen at the time, heard that we were being taken away and ran to the house. When she got there, Ronnie and Roy were already in the car, and I was screaming for her not to let them take me. But there wasn't anything she could do.

02 July 1964

Apprehended on behalf of Director of Child Welfare....

A green jeep brought us to a foster home on the Southside Hills, where we stayed for nearly a year. All I remember about this place was a very fat lady, and being in a crowded room with a lot of white cribs.

My father came to visit us on my birthday, bringing the largest red apple I'd ever seen. I remember him walking away from me on the train tracks. He said he was going away to find work and that he would come back to get me. He started walking too fast for me to catch up, and I began to cry, begging him to take me with him. That was the last I saw of my father for twelve years. My mother never visited.

On June 23, 1965, we were removed from our first foster home and placed with the Dinn's at 2 Norma's Avenue in Mount Pearl. I was five years old, Ronnie was around four, and Roy was about two. Mrs. Dinn had two children of her own, an older daughter who was married and lived away from home, and her adopted son, John, who was about my age.

When we arrived at the Dinns, we were shown a room upstairs where Mrs. Dinn said we were to sleep. She seemed friendly enough at first, but after the welfare officer left, we were sent down into the basement. She told me that Roy would remain upstairs because he was very small, but that Ronnie and I were to stay downstairs. The door closed behind me. I was puzzled and attempted to go upstairs, but was sent back down. I soon understood that this was where I was to spend my time. I huddled on the step, crying and whimpering to myself in the dark.

Family snapshots from Dereck's early life, before the separation of his family.

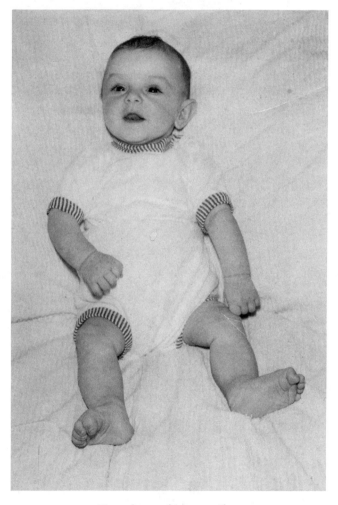

Dereck, age four months.

Mother, Marie O'Brien, with Dereck, age four months.

Marie and Dereck with friends.

23 June 1965

Removed on behalf of the Director of Child Welfare from Southside Road foster home to foster home at Norma's Avenue, Town of Mount Pearl....

[The applicants] would like to have a little boy around 5 years to be company for the little boy they adopted last year.... a new home...a well-constructed bungalow, detached, spacious back garden, front lawn....

14 May, 1970

I am pleased that Mr. and Mrs. ___ are continuing to provide excellent care and service for all their foster children.

Two

*T*hat first evening at the Dinns was the beginning of a four-year nightmare. In the beginning, it was Mrs. Dinn's screaming and shouting and her strange rules—like keeping us in the basement—that hurt and puzzled me. The daily beatings soon followed. Many times in those years I wondered why I was ever born. I couldn't understand why I was given away, or why the person who was supposed to take care of me was so cruel. I soon learned to hate that house and all—excepting the other foster children— who were in it.

Those other children came and went through the years—eleven placements over the period that I was there. But sharing the same fate didn't make us close. I barely remember most of them. They were usually very young, and lived upstairs. For the first year and a half, it was just Ronnie, Roy and myself living with the Dinn family.

A typical day at the Dinns, as in normal homes, began with breakfast. But mealtimes at this foster home were anything but normal. Although we spent most of our time confined to the basement, we were allowed into the kitchen to eat. We each had our own place around the table. By the time we were admitted upstairs, John had finished eating and would be seated at the head of the table, taunting us. We were not allowed to sit down. Not once did she permit me to sit in a chair like a human being. We would have to stand up around the table like cattle and eat this way.

The food was very poor. Breakfast was usually corn flakes and cold "hot" chocolate. I often had to eat my cereal dry. One morning I asked for milk. John began laughing and said, "Mom, Dereck wants mud on his corn flakes." I wasn't allowed to turn around to see what she was about to do, which was put dry cocoa powder on my cereal. She started laughing, and ordered me to eat it. When I did, she made me lick out the bowl.

Another morning, she made me put on a pair of red tights as punishment for tearing a pair of pants. She made me put the torn pants over them, and cut them off at the knees, so that the tights could be seen. She told me that I would have to go to school that way. I was on my way out the door, crying my heart out, before she called me back and let me change.

We all went to school together, except John, who took a taxi. Usually we walked, which took about an hour. Sometimes Mrs. Dinn gave us a ticket or ten cents to get the bus. I always favoured the money because I could spend it. This worked a couple of times, until she got wise to me and put a stop to it.

I'll never forget the first time I spent my ten cents on a small chocolate milk at lunchtime. I used to sit down and watch the kids at school buying things from the canteen and wished I could do the same. So one day, I used my bus fare to buy a chocolate milk. I wasn't worried about how I was going to get home until 2:30 when I realized that I had to do something. I went to my teacher and told her that I had lost my bus money. She gave me a ticket, and I couldn't believe that someone was being nice to me.

I couldn't wait after leaving the house in the morning to open my lunch box. It wasn't much—an apple, two cookies and half a sandwich—but I ate it like someone who was starving to death. If I had time when I walked to school in the morning, I would stop and shovel paths to people's houses. When I had finished, I would go to the door and tell them. Sometimes they would reward me with food. It was sort of a nice way to beg. That was something I was getting used to doing. I would never come right out and ask for food, but if it was offered, I rarely refused.

When lunch time came, I would be hungry again. I'd go to the lunch room and wait for the other kids to finish, so I could help clear the long wooden tables. When I emptied the garbage, I would pick out some kid's half-eaten sandwich and tuck it away for later. John saw me once and told his mother that I was taking sandwiches out of the garbage. I told her that I was taking them to feed the birds, but I got beaten anyway.

Chewing gum and candy that I found on the ground, full of rocks and sand, were a treat. I even stole food from a dog's dish once.

Walking home from school, we would take our time because we knew what was waiting for us at the end of the road. Shortly after Ronnie started school, he lost his bow-tie. That was surely a good reason to be afraid. I had a school chum who had a dog, and I thought maybe the dog could help us find it. It was a sheep dog, and at the time I didn't know he couldn't track down lost things. I thought all dogs could. It was dark before we finally gave up and headed home. When we got there, Mrs. Dinn was very upset. Not because she was worried, but because we weren't home on time.

When she asked why we were late, we froze because we knew we had to tell her. Ronnie confessed that he had lost his tie, and she started to hit him. She then started hitting me, because she said that I was responsible for Ronnie and that I should get some of what he was getting.

We were only permitted to wear our winter coats, caps and gloves to school. When we got home from school these items were put aside and the real rags were worn. One day at school, I lost one of my gloves; they were grey with leather palms and fingers. When I got home, I didn't tell her, but the next morning, she asked where my glove was. Because she found so many excuses for punishing us, I told her I left it in school. She became very mad and told me to make sure I brought it home that evening. I went through the lost and found box at school and was lucky enough to find a glove that was almost the same as the one I lost. She was waiting for me when I got home, and asked me where my gloves were. I showed her the two gloves, which looked enough alike that I fooled her. I was very relieved that this time I had gotten away without punishment.

Upon arriving home, we always had to knock and ask if we were allowed in. We were never allowed into the kitchen right away. She would make us take our clothes off in the porch and stand there until she opened the kitchen door. We could then go in and stand at our places around the table. Supper was worse than breakfast. I remember being given green stumps of cabbage, hard turnip and the fat from salt beet. Other times, table scraps were fed to us.

Mealtimes were unpredictable. One day, Ronnie and another boy, who both stood between the wall and the table, failed to answer when Mrs. Dinn asked them a question. She pushed the rest of us away and started to shove the table into the wall, ramming it up against both of their throats. I was afraid she was going to kill them before she stopped. The boys were screaming and gasping for air and their eyes were puffed out. Their necks were red and bruised, and they looked like they were about to faint.

There wasn't anything we could do except stand there and watch it all happen. If we made a move, God only knew what she would do to us. No one would take that chance. It was an awful feeling of helplessness. I think even she was worried when she saw their faces. She pulled back the table and continued on as though nothing had happened.

After meals, the routine was to go outside. I wouldn't dream of questioning what she told us to do, even if it was raining. I would put on my coat and boots, walk outside and stand out in the rain. There were times I was soaked to my skin and water filled my boots, but I didn't dare make a motion to come in. I just stood there and cried while the rain mixed with my tears, and no one could tell the difference. I spent untold periods of time waiting outside like a lifeless statue. Waiting for the call from her to come inside.

When it got dark, Ronnie, who was very young, would get scared and would want to go inside. We would huddle together under the steps to try to keep warm. She wanted us to stay somewhere in the yard where she could see us from the window. When she asked us what we were doing so close to the house, I replied that we were just playing. She would tell us to get out where she could see what we were doing. We obeyed, but when it got dark we would crawl back under the steps and wait.

In the winter, it got dark early. After being out for hours on end, Ronnie would plead for me to say the prayer. Whenever we were cold, hungry or outside like this, I would say, "Dear God, please put it in Mrs. Dinn's mind to call us in for the night, because we're cold and we want to come in." I said the same prayer when we were on the basement steps all night, half asleep and wanting to go to bed.

Even days when we had no school, like weekends and holidays, she woke us up very early in the morning, told us to get dressed and sent us outside—often without breakfast. I knew it was early, because there weren't any other children outside playing or any cars in the street. It didn't matter to her if it was cold and snowing or hot and sunny. I can remember having my pants frozen to my legs in winter and crying at the pain as my fingers began to warm up. My boots were too small, and my feet would cramp up inside them and become very cold. The clothes which we were given were not suitable for winter. We usually had a hood from a coat, summer pants and a windbreaker jacket.

I remember one day, Ronnie and I were out skating, and Ronnie asked Mrs. Dinn if he could come in, because his feet were cold. She told him he had to stay outdoors. The laces were frozen to his skates. When she finally let us in, I had to put the laces in my mouth to get the ice off, so I could untie them. I'll never forget what I saw when I peeled off his socks. His little feet were blue. Dark blue. I told Mrs. Dinn about it, and she said something along the lines of "Too bad." I had to put his feet under my shirt in order to get them warm again.

In the summer, we were never given any sun protection. I have fair skin and burn easily. Many times, I would blister and become sick. Mrs. Dinn wouldn't even give me a drink, much less take me to see a doctor. One day, I was very sick and my head was hurting badly. It hurt to open my eyes, and the light was unbearable. I went crying to Mrs. Dinn, because I didn't know what was wrong. When I asked for help, she drove me back outside and told me to stay there. When I went back out, I was so weak, I took a chance on laying down on the grass. She saw me, and screamed at me to get up. When I told her I couldn't, she came out and grabbed me, dragged me inside and threw me down the stairs. I hit my head on the floor and the door closed behind me. She never bothered to see if I was all right.

It was better in the basement that day, because at least I was cooler and there wasn't much light, so my eyes didn't hurt when I opened them. I was almost happy to know she wouldn't bother me. She never came down to the basement. If she wanted us, she would call out from the top of the stairs. It was only after they put a bedroom down there, she would come down to wake us up for school. Other than that, she stayed upstairs.

When we came in from outside, we had to sit on the basement steps for hours on end in the dark. There were times when we were asleep sitting up and Mr. Dinn came home with John after one of his cub meetings. The basement had a garage in it, and he would drive his car in there. When he opened the garage doors, it became even colder, but he wasn't in any hurry to close them. He and John would then come up the stairs, and we moved apart to let them pass. They would be laughing and talking as if we weren't there.

While I was living in Mt. Pearl, a new public library opened. John wanted to get a library card and so did I. Believe it or not, we were permitted to join the library and take out books. I was very proud to be allowed to have the power to take out books. But when we got home with them, Mrs. Dinn took them because we might tear them. The only time I saw the books was when I took them out and when it came time to bring them back. I think she wanted me to be stupid in order to give her a reason to hit me for not knowing my words in my school reader.

We would be called upstairs to do our home-work, with Mrs. Dinn standing over us with the stick that her budgie birds perched on in their cage. We called it the "bird stick." She would check my homework, and if any of it was wrong, she would bring me back to the table and tell me to turn around. I would stand with my back to her while she hit me on the neck, the back of my head, my face and my back with the stick. I think she enjoyed it when we did something wrong. Very rarely did she help me with my work. I remember a teacher who once said some awful things about my reading and other subjects. She said I was stupid, because I never got any of the answers right. Not much wonder. I was too worried about what was going to happen at home to concentrate on my school work.

I remember another incident when Mrs. Dinn "taught" me to tie my shoes. I used to slip out of my shoes after school, hoping I wouldn't untie the laces, because I didn't know how to tie them myself. Finally, a lace came undone. I stayed awake all that night wondering how to get by Mrs. Dinn in the morning without her seeing that my lace was undone. Unluckily for me, she saw it and told me to tie it.

"I don't know how," I said. "Would you show me?"

"Do it yourself," she told me.

I took the laces in my hands and attempted to tie them, but I kept getting them in knots. I was getting upset and began to cry. She told me to stop and got out the bird stick. When I saw what was coming, I begged her not to hit me, but she beat my hands until blood ran from my fingers.

I used to pray that God would take me out of this home and that my mother would come to get me, but my prayers went unanswered. I started to think that God couldn't do anything, and I gave up asking.

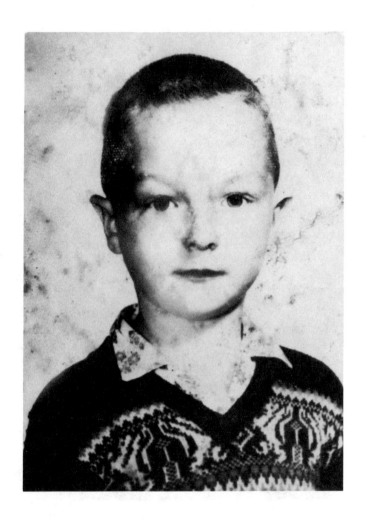

Dereck, grade one, living at the Dinn's.

Dereck's First Communion, about seven or eight years

13 February 1967

...committed temporarily to the care and custody of Director for a further term not yet determined....

Three

"Dogs aren't permitted to use the washroom in the house."

With that, Mrs. Dinn handed me a wad of toilet paper and sent me to the dump. It was always at night that this happened. I would ask to use the washroom, and she would reply that I made her beautiful house smell bad, and that I would have to go outdoors. After helping me with my coat, she pointed me towards the door and said, "Get outside and shit!" I left the house crying because it was dark and I was afraid. She warned me that she was watching to make sure I went all the way up to the dump.

For a small kid, it was a long walk. I walked very slowly, not looking back for fear that she was watching. I looked down at my feet, crying and jumping at every noise I heard. I looked at the houses that I passed, wondering if anyone knew what was happening to me, or if anyone would care if they did know.

I was afraid that when I got to the dump, there would be monsters and rats there. It was terrifying. I would rather soil my clothes and bear the consequences than walk to the dump at night. I had terrible pains from trying to hold my waste in.

Every now and then, we were allowed to use the indoor washroom, but mostly it was a forbidden place. I remember one evening, the bathroom window was steamed over. It must have been a Saturday evening, because that was when Mr. Dinn would take his bath. I wanted to use the bathroom really bad, but I waited for the steam to clear before I went in to ask. Unfortunately, I waited a little too long and started to do it in my pants. As I was walking across the kitchen floor on my way to the bathroom, a small piece of crap fell from my shorts. Mrs. Dinn stopped me and asked what it was. I said it was a crumpled piece of brown paper. She told me to pick it up and throw it in the garbage. Then she asked, "What is that smell?" By that time, I had already soiled my pants, but was too afraid to answer. She then grabbed me by the ears and started dragging me towards the bathroom.

"Why did you shit in your pants?" she wanted to know.

I was scared to come in the house without being told, let alone go to the washroom.

She made me strip naked and wait until she had decided what she was going to do with me. She came back to the bathroom and started to fill up the tub, as I stood there trembling. What happened next, I will never forget as long as I'm alive. She told me to get in the tub, but when I put my foot in, it was freezing. I told her this, but she insisted that I get in. Being more afraid of her than of the water, I did as she said. The cold water took my breath away. I guess I wasn't getting into the tub fast enough for her, so she forced me in and held me there. I was screaming at her, "Please, please, let me out! The water is too cold!" but she made me stay there.

She then left the washroom and went out around the corner, peeping in to see if I would try to get out. I didn't move, because I was afraid of what she might do to me. She left me there for some time. I remember my skin turning blue, and my teeth began to chatter. I was curled up in the tub, and I couldn't stop crying.

After a while, she took me out and drained the tub. She then started to fill the tub again. I begged her not to put me back in the cold water. Then I noticed that steam had started to cover the window and mirror.

I hoped that she was going to give me a warm bath, but she wasn't running any cold water to mix with the hot. She turned off the tap and started to put me in the tub. I pleaded with her again, but she forced me down into the water. When my skin touched the water, it was scalding hot, and I started to scream, but she made me sit down in it. She left me there for a while, as I tried to lift my bum and privates out of the hot water.

When she returned, she grabbed me by the ear and said, "That'll teach you to shit in your clothes again! You're not going to forget this lesson, are you?"

I don't think I'll ever forget what that woman did to me. She did the very same thing to my little brother once. I could hear him screaming, but there wasn't a damn thing I could do about it.

Because I was so afraid to ask to use the washroom, there were times I had no choice but to relieve myself in my clothes. Not only was it uncomfortable, but it made me feel bad about myself. I cursed myself for doing it, calling myself bad names and crying a lot.

She often left me for hours in this condition. After she had cleaned me, she would make me sit naked on the basement steps. Shivering with the cold, I sat there and wished my mother would come and get me and make me warm.

She told me I smelled like a dog and should be treated like one. She would stand at the doorway—she never came downstairs—calling, "Here, Fido!" I would walk up the steps as slowly as I could, not wanting to find out what she was about to do to me. She would have a half-smile on her face and I would have tears rolling down my cheeks.

She had dog names for all of us—Fido, Butch, etc. The first time she called me Fido, I insisted, "My name is Dereck, not Fido!" After she beat me enough, I answered to the name. She said I was only a dog anyway.

As if to prove her point, she would tie a rope around my neck, with the other end tied to a pipe that came out of the basement wall. I had to stand up and was not allowed to move until she called me by my dog name.

At least once or twice a week, I would get the "dog treatment." Sometimes it was punishment for soiling my clothes, other times it was just because the mood struck her. While the other children were upstairs eating, I would receive my food—left-over scraps—on a tin plate with no fork or knife. She would pass the scraps down to me, calling, "Here, Fido! Come get your supper, boy!"

In 1967, three new foster children arrived at the Dinns: two brothers and a sister. The girl didn't stay very long, but the boys were there longer than I was. They were the same ages as Ronnie and me, so they stayed in the basement with us. The older boy and I sat on a step that was close to the upstairs door, and the two younger boys had a step further down. This was to protect our younger brothers. Whenever Mrs. Dinn was in a bad mood and wanted to take it out on someone, she usually just grabbed whoever was closest to the door. There was never any conversation among us because we were afraid that she would hear us. We just sat in silence for hours and hours, with our knees folded to our chests and our heads tucked in our arms.

I rarely left the basement steps, for fear of being caught, but sometimes hunger or cold made me take a chance. I would cover myself with pink insulation to keep warm, or scrape the bottoms of the sugar bags that Mr. Dinn brought home from his job at the biscuit factory to get at the sugar that was wedged in there. I drank the small sips of pop left in empty bottles.

I was often thirsty. For some reason, Mrs. Dinn never gave us a drink of water. I think she was afraid we would wet the bed. At night when we brushed our teeth, I would sneak a drink from the container that held our toothbrushes, but my main source of drinking water was a pool on the basement floor. It was also a play toy. When the family went out and left us in the basement by ourselves, I would get off the steps and cross over to where the water was. After sneaking a quick drink, I played with little pieces of wood, pretending I was sailing a boat. As soon as I heard the car coming back in the driveway, I'd snatch the wood out of the pool and run back to my place on the stairs. Afraid that they would find the sticks on me, I dropped them between the steps. Something as simple as this would fill me with fear. Playing in a water pool was surely not permitted.

Once, there was a grey brick in the garage part of the basement. When the Dinns went out, I'd listen for the car to pull away, and then listen for movement upstairs. When I heard nothing, I went into the forbidden zone. One day, I was standing on the grey brick with my hands on the work bench, rocking the brick back and forth. I was pretending to be a cowboy riding his horse. I guess I went a little overboard, because the brick tipped over. Where should I fall, but in the puddle of water! You can't imagine my fear. I was wearing a pair of gold-coloured corduroy pants. When I hit the water, my bottom was soaked. I started to panic and began to cry, not knowing what to do. So I ran back to my step and began to pray that when Mrs. Dinn came home, she wouldn't call me up for supper. That was one time I would have gladly gone without!

When she did call, I knew I was doomed. When we were eating, I had my back to her, so she saw my wet pants right away. She asked what had happened. Fear set in, and I couldn't answer. She struck me, and I began to cry. I told her I had peed in my pants. I knew what kind of beating to expect for that, but I was afraid of what I might get if I told her I had been playing in the garage.

Sometimes the punishment was left for Mr. Dinn. He didn't take part in the beatings very often, but when he did, he made up for lost time. Mrs. Dinn would say, "Wait until Dad gets home," and it would instill me with terror. He got home late some nights, and his wife would make us stay up and wait for him. He would go upstairs without a word, as usual, and close the door behind him. I listened while she told him, Dereck did this or Dereck did that.

Before he had the door open, I was crying. When I looked up, he was in the porch, standing over me. He started to remove his belt, a wide black one that seemed to take forever to come off his waist. He then doubled it over, hitting his open hand with it, making a hollow, smacking sound. The other boys moved to avoid it. He asked me what I had done, but I was too afraid to answer. He then started hitting me over the head, driving me back down the stairs. When I reached the final step, there wasn't anywhere else to go. He made me drop my undershorts and started whipping my backside. I was screaming in pain. At six years of age, there's not a lot you can do to protect yourself from a man swinging a large leather belt. I remember the buckle hitting my private area and the piercing pain made my stomach sick. I was screaming, "Daddy, I'm sorry. I won't do it again." He whipped me even harder for talking. When he finished, he put his belt back through the loops on his pants and went back upstairs, wiping the sweat off his face.

I stood there with my hands against the wall, trembling and crying, afraid to move. I wouldn't get dressed because he never told me I could, and I was afraid he might come back down and beat me again for doing so without permission. After a long while, I figured he wasn't coming back, and bent over to pull up my pants. When I reached for them, they were wet. While he was beating me, I'd peed all over them. He hit me so hard, and I was so scared, I couldn't help it. The other boys told me to get dressed, but my pants were hurting my legs and my behind. I finally managed to pull them up and made my way back to my step after what seemed an endless climb.

"Is it hard sitting down?" my brother asked me.

I don't know which hurt worse sometimes, the pain or the humiliation.

July 2, 1968

Dear Sir;

This foster home is now in its fourth year of operation. I am pleased to report that Mr. and Mrs. (censored) are continuing to provide excellent care for the foster children in their home. These people have a genuine love of children and are honorably motivated. They get a great feeling of satisfaction in caring for unfortunate children. On many occasions they provide services over that which is normally expected.... This warmth and feeling is always evident and children placed in this home adjust extremely well. ...we feel that all children placed in this home benefit greatly from her service.

...this is in my opinion, the ideal foster family and one of our very best homes.

(from a welfare officer's report released to the Hughes Inquiry in regards to allegations made against the Dinn's foster home in Mount Pearl)

Four

*P*laying and playmates were almost unknown to us. The Dinn's yard had a set of swings, a glider and a slide, but we were never allowed to use them. They were for their son John. For toys, we took flat rocks and painted them with a mixture of crushed soft rock and spit. These were our cars and trucks. John had a Batman car that I loved and wished many times to own. My wife gave me one for my thirtieth birthday.

We had none of the usual childhood heroes— no Santa Claus, no tooth fairy, no hockey stars. We weren't allowed to watch television, so I was always teased at school for not knowing the names of hockey players.

A very nice lady once gave me a toy hockey player. She gave it to me when I told her it was my birthday. When Mrs. Dinn found out, she made me bring it back, but the lady said, "That's all right, you keep it anyway."

I was so happy that I was to have a toy of my own! I returned, beaming, to tell Mrs. Dinn. She took it and broke it. The only thing I was ever allowed to keep was a tiny crucifix that glowed in the dark, which I received for my first communion. I still have a piece of it today, the only memento I have from that foster home.

When John's friends came around, we had to stay in a different part of the garden. We weren't allowed to speak to them at all.

There was a young boy named Brucie, who lived next door. He used to ask us to come over the fence and play, but we always refused. Mrs. Dinn would beat us if we ever left the back yard. She always had the curtains open wide enough to keep an eye on us.

Brucie was digging in his yard one day, playing. I wandered over to the fence to ask him what he was doing. He was talking to me when I heard a rap on the window. I looked up to see Mrs. Dinn. She looked very angry and was motioning for me to come in. I knew what was about to happen. With every step I took towards the door, I could hear my heart pounding in my ears. When I got inside, she hit me on top of my head with her knuckles and told me never to disobey her again. I came back out, crying. Brucie didn't bother to ask me what happened—he already knew.

I did have a bike, a hand-me-down from John. I had received some money in the mail for Christmas one year. I think it was around thirty dollars. To a six-year-old kid, that seemed like a thousand. All the kids were going around on bikes, and I told Mrs. Dinn I wanted a banana bike. She wrote up the order, and I was so proud. I went to school telling all the kids that I was getting a banana bike for Christmas. The bike came, all right, but it was for John. I was told that his sister had bought it for him. When I asked John for a ride on it, his mother said, "Don't ride on John's bike. You'll make the seat stink." She gave me his old one, saying it was only garbage anyway.

I wasn't allowed to store my bike in the basement when it rained. It was kept outside next to the chimney, even in the winter. One day when I went outside, my bike couldn't be seen. It was covered with snow, and when I uncovered it, I saw that the chain had started to rust and wouldn't go around the flywheel. I had never owned very much, and this bike, hard as it looked, was still my bike. So I took it under the backsteps and turned it upside down to get the wheels moving. When I finally got them turning, my brother Ronnie, not knowing the danger, put his little hand into the moving flywheel and chain. He started screaming and blood was flying everywhere. When I saw the mess his hand was in, I became very frightened. I managed to remove his hand from the tangle of the bike, but I'm sure you could see the bones in his knuckles. I ran inside—after knocking—and told Mrs. Dinn what had happened. She asked to see his hand. When he took it from his pocket, it was covered with wood and dirt from the coat's lining. I almost got sick. Mrs. Dinn looked at it, cleaned it and sent him back outside.

Ronnie was wearing a brown wool coat with no hood, which was very thin. He was in a lot of pain, and his hand was still bleeding. It started to seep through the lining of his coat, and then through the outer material, turning it a very dark colour. It's a wonder he didn't lose his fingers, because it was very cold and he was losing a lot of blood. We didn't have any mittens to wear. He was crying and complaining of the cold, so I opened my jacket and wrapped both of us in it. I can't remember how long we stayed like that, but it was dark before she called us in.

Her son was a person I really began to hate. He made us suffer for his own amusement. He would make us run around the back yard because he wanted to see if we would fall down. We did as he told us, because he could get us in trouble with his parents.

One afternoon, we were all outside kicking around an old brown ball, when Ronnie kicked it through the basement window. You could see the colour drain from his face and fear come into his eyes. In no time, John was running for the house, telling his mother that Ronnie had broken the window. When he came back out, she was right behind him. I stepped in front of Ronnie and said it was me who had kicked the ball and broken the window. John said it was Ronnie, but I insisted. I told her that I was sorry, and she said, "You'll be sorry all right. Just wait until your dad gets home."

I hated that because he wasn't my dad, but they insisted on being called Mom and Dad.

She ordered me inside and sent me to the basement with a few smacks on the top of my head. I was there until Mr. Dinn came home. She took great pride in telling him what had happened. I heard him cross the kitchen floor to the basement door. He walked past me, and I jumped in fear. He went to the broken window, examining it for a couple of minutes and then he called me. I walked towards him slowly. Believe me, I wasn't in any rush for what was about to come. He then picked me up by my feet off the floor and asked me why I had broken his window. I told him I had kicked the ball too hard and I was sorry. He then dropped me to the hard floor and started kicking me. After three or four kicks, he stormed to his workbench to get some tools to fix the window. He didn't hit me again that night, but for a long time after, I wasn't permitted outside to play, and I was kept locked up in the basement for days.

John was treated the way I thought children were supposed to be treated. He had candy and toys and friends—things that we could only dream of. When Mr. Dinn took everyone out for a drive, he would stop into a store and come back out with three ice cream cones, with white paper on the cone and wax paper over the top to protect them from dirt and melting. He would pass one to Mrs. Dinn, one to John, and keep one for himself. The rest of us sat in the back seat, drooling and trying to keep back the tears. I tried not to look at the ice cream, gazing out the window in an effort to keep my mind off it.

Things like that were common. John returned from a shopping trip one day with something that really upset me. I had always wanted a catcher's mitt, because I was the catcher for the little league baseball team and was always borrowing a mitt. I asked Mrs. Dinn many times to buy me one for my birthday, but was always disappointed. When John came down the hallway, punching his fist into the brand-new catcher's mitt, I wanted to hit him; he knew how much I wanted one. To rub salt into the wound, he had a new ball and bat as well. He was never very good at playing ball, and his parents knew he wasn't going to use the new equipment, but he got it anyway. I asked if I could try the mitt on, but he said my hands were never to touch it. You'd have thought he was going to catch something from me.

I finally convinced him to have a game of baseball in the back yard. He still wanted to be catcher, which was okay by me, because when it was my turn at bat, I smacked his new ball over the fence and into the neighbour's yard! He ran into the house crying to his mother. I knew she would beat me, but I almost didn't mind! Sure enough, she sent me over the fence to find the ball, then smacked me around a bit, and that was the last I ever saw of the black catcher's mitt. John never brought it or the baseball and bat out again.

In a way, I can't blame him for being the way he was. He was a product of his environment, after all, and he watched his mother cause us pain every single day.

She sometimes took us shopping together. In Mount Pearl there was a square with several small stores. She and John would go inside and leave me outside, standing by a black steel post. She told me not to move until she came out. I don't know why she didn't want me to come in the stores with her.

Adults would walk past and remark how polite I was, saying to their own children, "Why can't you be more like that little boy?" Little did they know why I was polite and didn't move. I remember John came out one day with a bottle of root beer. He was drinking from a straw. She never gave me anything, even though she knew I was thirsty. When John had his fill, he began spitting the drink on the ground. He knew that I wanted some, but he would rather spit it out than share it with me.

When Mrs. Dinn was finished her shopping, we would walk home. She made me walk in front. Maybe she was afraid that I would run away. Nothing could have been further from my mind. We were too terrified to cross over to the wrong side of the garden, let alone run away.

"Family" outings were always like that. The abuse was never left behind at the house. I remember sitting with Mr. Dinn by the fountain at the mall one day, and being pinched very hard when I reached to pick up a penny.

Every Christmas, there was a Santa Claus who came to the parking lot of a local school. He would throw small bags of candy into the crowd, and parents would catch them to give to their children. Mr. Dinn used to take me and John there. He would catch the little brown paper bags and give them to John. Any extra ones Mr. Dinn caught, he put into his own pocket. He never gave me one, although his pockets were stuffed. When Santa began to move away, people headed home. We were walking across the parking lot one time, when I saw a bag that had fallen to the ground. It was ripped, and the treats were all over the ground. I bent over and picked them up. Mr. Dinn didn't see me. I put some of the candy in my pocket, and some in my mouth. When I got home, I shared it with Ronnie. To my surprise, there was a piece of pink bubble gum that no one had chewed before—a rare treat! I chewed a piece off, and gave some to Ronnie. That piece of gum lasted for about two weeks. I never chewed it around Mrs. Dinn, because I figured it was reason enough for her to hit me. I chewed it in the basement, and when I went out, I stuck it under my step. When I came back in, I would have a chew. This went on until it had turned to water in my mouth. Gum and candy were something other kids had—something I could only wish for—and for me, wishes never came true.

One day, I found a nickel when I was on my way to the store for Mrs. Dinn. It was between the store's steps, and on my way out, I reached down and picked it up. I didn't go back in the store and spend it, because I was afraid the lady who ran it would telephone Mrs. Dinn and tell her I had money. I was afraid of adults. I thought that they all knew each other. So I kept it and showed it to Ronnie as soon as I got home. When he was passing it back, it slipped through his fingers and fell between the steps. I was beside myself. I was afraid that if I chanced going down to get it, she would open the door and see that I wasn't where I was supposed to be. I comforted myself with the knowledge that it was safe where it was.

Sometime later, John came down into the basement, poking around, and found the nickel. He picked it up and teased me with it. I wouldn't dare say that it was mine, because I would have to explain where I had gotten it. I thought that if I told the truth, Mrs. Dinn wouldn't believe me and would ask where I had stolen it. So John kept the nickel, and I said nothing. It was just one more setback.

What everyone else took for granted, I could only wish for. No toys, no friends and very little comfort. Mrs. Dinn always told me that I was never wanted, never loved, and that the only reason I was there was that she was getting paid for keeping me. I never heard the words, "How are you? Did you have a nice day?" or "I love you." I never knew what it was like to be held when I was sick, or cheered up when I was feeling bad.

Even Christmas was not much different from any other day. The only indication that it was a special occasion was a small plastic bag containing a few grapes and couple of candies which we would receive. We were never allowed to spend Christmas Day upstairs. In a way, we were glad that Mrs. Dinn was too preoccupied to bother with us.

The first time I saw a Christmas tree in that house, was when there was a babysitter with us who had told us to come upstairs. We turned down the offer, explaining that it wasn't permitted, but she insisted that it was okay. We went up, and I saw the tree, white with red bulbs. We sat down in the living room and she turned on the television. I felt completely out of place. We never moved or took our eyes off the screen.

When Mrs. Dinn came home, she somehow found out that we had been upstairs. She beat us and told us never to sit on her sofa again.

She was totally immune to the holiday spirit. Coming home from school one day for Christmas holidays, I kicked something in the snow. I picked it up, wiped it off and saw that it was a Christmas ornament. It was diamond-shaped and sparkled when it caught the light. I decided I would give it to Mrs. Dinn. She threw it in the garbage and told me never to bring anything into the house again.

It was the same when I brought home projects from school. I was put down and told that a baby could do better. You can imagine how highly I began to think of myself. I vividly recall thinking about throwing myself in front of a car or bus in hopes of being killed, and then remembering that there would be no one to look out for my brothers if I did so.

I think I was all of seven or eight years old.

08 July 1968

...ordered committed permanently to the care and custody of Director of Child Welfare.

I don't know the reason we were taken from Mrs. Dinn's; I only remember my shocked disbelief. I thought I would have to spend the rest of my life with her. I thought at first that it must be a joke, but my doubts soon gave way to happiness. I didn't dare show it, however, in case something went wrong.

Ronnie and I were outfitted in new clothes. He soiled his pants at least three times that day, just to get back at Mrs. Dinn. He knew she would have to change them because the welfare officer was arriving any time!

I waited to go, still not quite able to believe that I was being set free. I wasn't going to have to cry at her hands anymore. I wouldn't have to beg for her to stop hitting me anymore. I would never have to walk to the dump again. It was staggering.

However, there were two sad notes to an otherwise happy day. I thought that it was my mother and father who were coming to get me at last. When the welfare officer arrived, I was crushed to realize that this was not to be, and that I wasn't going home.

The other heartache was having to leave my youngest brother, Roy, behind. For some reason, he was to stay. I'll never forget the walk from the front door to the car. I looked back to see him standing in the doorway. He was very small and didn't even come up to Mrs. Dinn's waist. I never knew what happened in that house after I left, but I know in my own heart and soul that it never got any better.

31 July 1969

*Removed on behalf of Director of Child Welfare from Norma's Ave.,
Town of Mount Pearl foster home and placed in foster home at
O'Donnell's, St. Mary's Bay....*

Five

*F*rom hell to heaven is the only way I can explain what lay ahead. We lived with Mrs. Hanlon in a community called O'Donnell's, St. Mary's Bay, for a brief but wonderful year.

I remember the day we arrived at a small, two-bedroom house in a field. Mrs. Hanlon wasn't at home, having gone to St. John's to do some shopping. It was around suppertime and her son, Peter, who was twelve or thirteen at the time, had salt fish and boiled potatoes cooked. He told us supper was ready and invited us to have some. He put a large white plate on the table and placed a piece of fish and two large potatoes on it. I assumed that it was to be shared between myself and Ronnie and was surprised when he put down another plate. We looked at each other, not believing our eyes—a plateful each.

We had begun to eat when Peter asked why we were standing up. I told him that we weren't allowed to sit at the table. He told me, "In this house everyone is treated the same; you sit down for meals and you eat as much as you want so long as you don't waste it."

Kenneth, another son, was also present the night we arrived. He was around seventeen at the time. He didn't say much. I remember he was amazed at the way we stood at the table to eat. He had never seen anyone stand at meals before.

We were shown a room that we were to share with Kenneth and Peter. They shared one bed, and Ronnie and I shared another. The room was just large enough for the beds and a chest of drawers where our clothes were kept.

Mrs. Hanlon came home after supper. I remember seeing an older lady with soft eyes and a wonderful smile. I knew right away that things were going to be different with her. She was a small person, with a special glow about her. She was soft-spoken and rarely raised her voice. She would have been a wonderful mother for us. She asked us if we had eaten, and if we knew where our rooms were, and the rest just fell into place from there.

Mr. Hanlon wasn't there when we first arrived. He spent most of his time in Labrador City where he worked at the iron ore mines. When I met him later, he struck me as being a nervous person who spent most of his time sitting in the rocking chair. He never spent any time with us, and he very rarely spoke to us.

Mrs. Hanlon had six more children. Her sons, Ralph and Gus, went to work with their father in Labrador City and weren't around much. There was another son that I never met, and one whose name I don't remember. There were two daughters, Hanna and Margaret, who were married and only came home for visits.

This woman, who I finally called Mom, was very special, kind and understanding. She never smacked me or made me feel bad; she never hurt my feelings. Whatever she had to give she gave it, never questioning my actions.

She was always concerned with how we were doing in school and how we felt we were being treated in her house. I had chores to do, but I didn't mind doing them. One of my chores was bringing in water, because the house didn't have running water. I also helped with the firewood and cleaning up around the door. She had rules, but they were rules that I had no problem obeying.

I finally felt free. I could run through the fields and walk on the beach picking up driftwood every Saturday morning. Ronnie and I brought home to Mrs. Hanlon many "treasures" we found washed up on the beach. She went along with us and said how wonderful these things were, knowing that they were just junk. She always took the time to listen to our stories. She always had time to hug us and help us with our homework.

One time I remember she bought me and Ronnie new hip rubbers. We were really excited and ran for the salt water, thinking we could go to our waist without getting wet. We soon found out we were wrong. Mrs. Hanlon just laughed about it and told us the difference.

Kenneth had a soft spot for Ronnie. I think this was because Ronnie was small and shy. Ken used to spend a lot of time with him making go-carts and carving out wooden guns, and playing with both of us. Peter got kind of jealous, which was understandable, because he was the youngest and we were getting a lot of attention.

On one side of the house, separated by a fence, lived Mr. Hanlon's brother and his family. It was a place we visited almost every day, because they had children around the same age as myself and Ronnie who we played with. They were the first real playmates we ever had.

On the other side lived an elderly lady who lived alone and kept sheep. Ronnie and I used to call the sheep over to the fence and feed them. It was the closest I had ever come to a farm animal. I saved potato peels and cabbage scraps for them. I remember there was one little lamb we used to call Fleecy.

When we came to O' Donnell's, I was going into grade five, and Ronnie was going into the second grade. The kids at school were curious about us at first. They wanted to know where we came from and why we were there. After a while, we were more or less accepted, but they always knew us as the welfare kids.

Mrs. Hanlon reassured us that we belonged. She took us to church and seemed to feel proud that we were with her. Whenever she went out visiting she brought us along with her. We were never hungry, never cold and never mistreated. It was as if we had truly become part of her family.

The food at Hanlon's was always good—the kind of food that outport families have: salt fish, meat and potatoes. There was always plenty, and usually there was dessert, such as homemade pies, cookies and jams. For the first time in my life I didn't have to eat with my fingers, and I could ask for more without receiving a smack in the face.

I was given things that I had only dreamed about before. We were given money to go to the store to buy treats for ourselves. We had the freedom to run, play, and just be kids—something I had never experienced up to that point.

I lived with Mrs. Hanlon from July 31, 1969, until August 25, 1970. They were about the most wonderful thirteen months of my life. However, the happiness was short-lived.

One day, Mrs. Hanlon sat me and Ronnie down and held our hands while she told us that she had to go away to Toronto. She was having an operation on her eyes, and we had to go live with someone else. She seemed sad and told us that she would bring us back to live with her when she was well again. But in the pit of my stomach, I felt that it was not to be. I was used to things coming to an end; used to things not working out.

The day we left, I cried and held onto Mrs. Hanlon, begging her not to let me go. I remember walking down the path towards the road, kicking the small beach rocks beneath my feet, as tears streamed down my face. I knew that I would never be coming back there.

We were then transferred to another foster home in Admiral's Beach, which was about seven miles from O'Donnell's. Once again, my world had come crashing down.

I don't have any bad memories of Mrs. Hanlon; just the wonderful feeling of not worrying about when the next beating was coming, and not being afraid to speak. She was the only real mom I ever had. I even started to write my name as Dereck Hanlon on my school books. I thought that I would live with her forever. I finally felt that I belonged to someone. One year wasn't enough for a small boy who had just begun to feel cared for and loved.

To end this chapter, I want to thank Mom Hanlon for that wonderful year; for sharing her home, her family and her love, and for caring about a foster child as if he were her own.

Ronnie and Dereck at Mrs. Hanlon's.

25 August 1970

...on behalf of Director of Child Welfare...placed in foster home at Admiral's Beach, St. Mary's Bay....

Six

We went to the foster home in Admiral's Beach in the summer of 1970 when I was nine years old. This foster home was run by Mrs. Dalton and was nice for about a month, although from the day we went there we knew we weren't wanted. Mrs. Dalton said to the welfare officer, "I'll take them, I suppose, even though I wanted two girls."

Mrs. Dalton would kiss me on the head, tuck me in and say good night. This soon ended and was replaced by name-calling. The woman's daughters would call both of us names such as Spock, Ugly-face and many more, often they would flick my ears. They would make us wait until they had finished eating before we were allowed to eat at the table. We had to stay outdoors until we were called in for meals. We were then sent outside again, and we weren't allowed to come in until we were called. Mr. Dalton let us go into his shed when we wanted to.

When we were called to meals, we were never given a choice of food or seconds. We could not help ourselves to anything. Her children would be given bedtime snacks. Sometimes we would be given bread and molasses, most of the time, nothing. If I asked for something more to eat, I was told I didn't need it and to get to bed.

The house was an old two-story type which was very cold in the wintertime. The room we were given first was very nice, just one bed for me and my brother. Shortly after we arrived, this room was taken from us and given to one of her older children. We were moved into a smaller room with another bed, one that two of her other daughters shared. There was no door and the window frame had large holes in it. I remember stuffing an old rag into the hole, and the ice on the window sill was at least half an inch thick. We never had any heat and, worse than that, we never had a private place to ourselves.

Once, on a trip to St. John's, Mrs. Dalton brought home lettuce, tomatoes and grapes, items not sold in the small corner store in Admiral's Beach. Everyone was given a bowl of grapes, except me. I was given about six on a vine. I became upset and started to cry. Anyway, I peeled each grape before I ate it and savoured every one.

I wanted to taste the lettuce, although I knew Mrs. Dalton would be watching to see how long it lasted. The next day, I watched her daughters make a salad with it—I'd never seen that before—and I did the same. Later that night, I was sitting in the living room when she came in, screaming, demanding to know who had eaten all of her lettuce. Everyone had eaten some, but because I had eaten the last of it she decided I was to blame. She told me I couldn't eat everything and she struck me on the top of my head with her knuckles. I started to cry. Everyone laughed at me, jeering and making fun. I guess because I was rather big for my age, they thought I was too big to have my feelings hurt, or they didn't take time to consider what they were doing. I stormed out of the room and went upstairs to get away from everyone and to ponder the same old question: why did my mother give me up?

As a foster child, it was very difficult for me to fit in with other people. The foster children in the area were easy to identify—we had the most outdated haircuts and the worst clothes. People addressed me by saying, "Oh, you're that welfare boy that lives at Elizabeth's."

In the era of long hair, the seventies, I was never allowed to let my hair grow. The Dalton's would shave my hair off with the hand clippers, taking pieces of hair out and scarring my head. This also gave the kids at school something else to laugh at and another reason to make fun of me. I felt hurt and very upset when girls my age wouldn't have anything to do with me. Mrs. Dalton made sure I wasn't allowed to go to school dances. She always told me that I was never old enough to attend. If I was twelve, she would say that I had to be thirteen to go to dances. When her daughters went, they would make fun of me because they knew I really was old enough to go.

I wasn't allowed to leave the grounds or walk the streets with my friends. When they sang out to me, I'd pretend not to hear them and then walk away. When my friends went off swimming, they would come and ask me to go with them, but I was never allowed. I made up excuses and lies because I wasn't permitted to hang around with them. Even though there wasn't a fence around the yard, I knew where my boundary was and I never tested it to see if I could go any further. I continually asked to be able to go with them, but the answer was always no. After a while I stopped asking. I was never allowed to play street hockey and could only watch from the yard, hoping that some day she would let me play with my friends. I really wanted to play when they were out in the night under the street light. It doesn't seem like much, but to me it was very important.

My foster uncle and aunt, one of Mr. Dalton's brothers and his wife, lived next door. I remember once I was outside making a hockey stick in Uncle Alban's shed when I cut my leg very badly with the saw. All I was worried about was how I was going to explain the rip in my pants. Aunt Phil came out, saw my leg, brought me inside and wrapped it. Because I was crying, she asked me if I was in pain. I said no. When she asked me why I was crying, I told her I was afraid of what was going to happen to me when my foster mother saw my pants.

As a young boy, I missed out on a lot of things: father and son banquets, clubs, going for walks in the park and playing on the swings—things I do now with my own children. Going for ice cream, and doing simple things like kicking a ball around or playing catch. Having someone to tell me stories or tell of things that happened long ago. Going fishing.

To justify my crew cut, I joined the army cadets, where everyone had short hair. Cadets gave me a chance to be a part of something and a chance to go on trips. I took great pride in caring for my uniform and I tried my best to be a good cadet.

I was also very proud of my work as an altar boy. I had become involved with the church as a means of getting some time alone, away from the house. Even when I wasn't helping with mass, I'd go to church, not to pray but to be by myself. I became a very good altar boy and helped to serve mass many times, even when other altar boys had lost interest in it. On the altar, I felt that I was worth something; that I was above the name-calling and sneers. I was not only proud, but I felt better than the members of my foster home. After all, they had to look up to me when they received Holy Communion.

The priest was always friendly. Whenever he needed someone to serve mass, he requested that I be the one to do it. This made me feel very proud. It was something that I was good at, and someone respected me for doing it. This was also the one place I didn't need Mrs. Dalton's permission to come to. I could come and go as I pleased, and I did just that.

When I was eleven years old, I was put to work at the fish plant for the summer, working sometimes fourteen to eighteen hours a day, wheeling in fish. I was not very strong, and I hurt my back badly. I asked to see a doctor, but was never allowed to go for treatment. I had to continue working in pain. When I received my pay cheque, I had to bring it home and hand it over to Mrs. Dalton. She said she was putting it in a savings account for me to have later. Later never came; she took all of my money and kept it for herself.

One morning, I was making breakfast for her younger daughter. I was toasting bread (I was never allowed to have toast) when the toaster broke. Mrs. Dalton said that a new toaster would have to come from my savings. Many times, she went to St. John's, returning with new clothes for her and her daughters, but nothing for me.

"I bought this from the money that was in your account," she used to say.

Working at the fish plant, my lips and hands became blistered and cracked. The skin on my knuckles split, and it was very painful when I had to put them in the cold salt water. I asked for some cream to put on them, but Mrs. Dalton refused, saying that it would make me tough.

One of her daughters, who was married and living at home with her child, said that the reason my lips and hands were so sore was because I had been stealing cans of custard from her baby. To be accused of stealing food from a child was about as much as I could take. I asked her to prove it, and she said that someone had seen me eating something on my way to work and throwing something in the ditch. This was reason enough to blame me! I put that child to bed and sang her to sleep more often than her own mother did when she was living there. When the baby woke up in the middle of the night, I was the one who got up and made the bottle. I was furious that her mother would think such a thing.

When I came home from work, I wasn't permitted to change in the house. I had to use the shed. This I could understand, because after working with fish all day long, my clothes sure didn't smell very nice. But I had to wear the same clothes for five or six days running, without having them washed. By week's end, my pants could stand up by themselves.

I also had to eat my meals out in the porch when I was working, because Mrs. Dalton said that I made the house smell. My clothes were dirty but she had no problem with taking my clean money from me.

The guys I worked with often teased me about the fact that I never had any money and called me a fool for handing over my pay cheque. The boys went to the store, where they had tabs, and charged things until they got paid. I was dared to do the same, so I opened a tab, even though the store owner, who was related to my foster mother, questioned me and asked how I would pay for it. I told him not to worry, but I couldn't pay it, of course. Some time later, when I went back to this foster home to visit Ronnie, I was presented with the bill which I still owed.

Whenever she had raffle tickets to sell, Mrs. Dalton sent me door-to-door selling them. I walked from one end of the settlement to the other, covering about three or four miles. She never said, "Thank you," or "Here's something for yourself." I felt like a bum going from house to house. She never asked her own children to do it.

Mr. Dalton's brother, Gus, and his wife were very nice people too, as nice as Uncle Alban and Aunt Phil. One day, Uncle Gus's water pipes froze, so I spent the entire day bringing water to his house in pails. He gave me five dollars for my trouble, which was a lot of money. I felt good, knowing that I had money in my pocket. When I got home, Mrs. Dalton asked how much money Uncle Gus had given me. I told her, and she told me to hand it over. She took my money and put it on top of the fridge. I didn't think to question it.

When Mr. Dalton came home, he asked the same question: how much money had Uncle Gus given me? I told him, but he knew something was wrong by the way I answered him. He asked me about it, and I told him that his wife had taken my money. He became very upset and asked her why she had taken it. She told him that I should save it for school supplies.

"That's no reason to take his money," he said, giving it back to me.

As soon as he left the room, Mrs. Dalton hit me on the top of my head with her fist. I started to cry, and she called me names.

Mr. Dalton was kind, but rarely interfered. His wife always did an about-face when he was around. The same thing happened in the presence of the boarder who was living there. I think she was afraid to let anyone see her the way she really was.

Mr. Dalton was a sick man, in and out of the hospital with stomach problems, so he was at home quite often. I spent a lot of time with him. He was a heavy smoker and he kept his smokes out in the pantry. He had to know that his cigarettes were disappearing faster than they should have been. By this time, I was smoking heavily myself.

When he went to sleep, I'd go through his pockets, looking for change. He was always nice to me and stealing from him never felt right, but that still didn't stop me.

The Dalton's son-in-law, Len, was also very nice to me. He took me fishing in his boat. He bought me things and took me with him whenever he went for a drive. I'll never forget his kindness.

I lived with Mrs. Dalton, I often dreamed of returning to Mrs. Hanlon's to live, but after a while I knew that this was never going to happen. At first, my brother Ronnie was very unhappy living with Mrs. Dalton, because for the first time he felt that he had been taken away from his real mother. I felt the same. Many times Ronnie would run away and go back to Mrs. Hanlon's in hopes that she would take us back. We never understood why such an awful thing had happened to such a wonderful woman.

Ronnie later came to like living at the Dalton's, and he was well-treated there. I suppose his being younger and smaller made him a novelty, whereas my being older and big for my age just made me useful for work. Whatever the reason, they were kind to him, and the only friends he can remember from childhood are those from Admiral's Beach.

I have no kind memories of Mrs. Dalton. One night when I was living there, I woke up to the sound of someone screaming. I jumped out of bed to go see what was happening, but the youngest daughter came into our room, crying that her father had scalded her mother's arm with hot water. She seemed surprised that I wasn't as upset as she was.

"What for?" I said. I wasn't about to shed a tear over a woman I never cared for.

The girl started screaming at me. "If it wasn't for my mother, you'd be in some foster home where nobody cared about you!" she said.

I told her I'd already been in one, and that I couldn't give a damn where I went next, because I surely wasn't wanted in her house.

Mrs. Dalton's arm turned out to be burned very badly, and she needed skin grafting, which meant many visits to the hospital in St. John's. I was happy when she was gone.

...a happy atmosphere always pervades this home and all members of the family interact well with each other.

...from a child welfare report on Dalton's foster home, 1973.

While we were living in Admiral's Beach, an adoptive home was found for Ronnie and me. We were told that a well-to-do couple in Ontario was going to adopt us, and that we would live on their farm. I understood that Roy was coming with us. Everything was all but final when a social worker took us to see Roy at the Dinn's.

It was a very brief visit, and the social worker supervised it, but it was scary all the same. I remember Mrs. Dinn standing in the background. As if that were not bad enough, it slowly began to dawn on me what this visit was about: we were there to say goodbye to Roy. As soon as we left, I demanded to know if Roy was going to be adopted with us. The social worker explained that the couple in Ontario only wanted two boys.

I kicked up a stink, threatening to run away and behave badly if they made us go without Roy. The adoption fell through.

In April of 1973, I told a visiting welfare officer about what had happened to us at Mrs. Dinn's. I told her the names of the people who had lived there, and about the things that had gone on there during our stay. She began writing. I remember that her facial expression was one of disbelief. It was as if she couldn't believe what I was telling her.

The report was never acted on. Mrs. Dinn continued to operate a foster home at 2 Norma's Avenue until 1975 and was much praised for her efforts by the department of social services.

It was not the last time that someone tried to blow the whistle on Mrs. Dinn. In recent years, I met a woman who took Mrs. Dinn's foster children into her foster home for a while when Mrs. Dinn was sick. She became very fond of the children. My brother, Roy, was among them. When it came time for them to return to Mrs. Dinn's, they became very upset. She told me that they ran upstairs and crawled under the bed, screaming and crying. The woman's son had to drag them into the waiting taxi. Even the driver knew that something was wrong.

She phoned the department of child welfare and reported the incident, urging them to remove the children from Mrs. Dinn's foster home. Something must have been amiss for these kids to become so upset at the thought of returning. Her call fell on deaf ears. The welfare people didn't want to rock the boat.

As far as I'm concerned, to the welfare department, we were just a number on a file, and with that number came payment for our care. The welfare officers would come every now and then and have a cup of tea with the foster parents, smile a lot, and go on to the next house. They never looked for any sign that something was wrong. When we lived at Mrs. Dinn's, she would dress us up in new clothes, stand us up and wait for the welfare officer to come. She would also warn us not to say a word when we were asked questions. The welfare officer would sit down; we would stand next to her. She would speak to us, say, "My, your hair is so nice," or "Oh, what a nice outfit you're wearing." Mrs. Dinn was asked if the children were behaving themselves and if they were causing her any problems. It seems they were more concerned about her than they were about our welfare. The officer never took the time to look beyond the basement door to see where the real hell hole existed.

My brothers and I were not the only children overlooked by the system. How many more are there that haven't been heard from? Who gave a damn how we were being treated? Who gave a damn for our physical or emotional well-being? It seems that things had to pass the bursting point before anyone would listen. Some ears are opened now, but in our case the damage has been done.

I don't wish to sound mean or cruel. What's happened to me hasn't made me either of those things. But I want someone to tell me why nothing was ever done. Did they think that because I was young, I was lying? Did they think that these things weren't happening? Or maybe it was just easier to lose the report for seventeen years and hope to never see it again. Perhaps they felt it was better not to act, because they didn't want to make themselves look bad. Because they were afraid of what they might find at 2 Norma's Avenue, if they opened the hornet's nest.

Seven

I could not continue to live at the foster home in Admiral's Beach and requested to be removed from there. The only place left to go was Mount Cashel.

On January 4, 1973, Ronnie and I were driven to the orphanage at 67 Torbay Road in St. John's. Ronnie was nine and I was eleven or twelve. The welfare officer pointed it out as we approached.

"There is your new home," she said.

We looked up and saw this big, grey, cold-looking building and our first reaction was "oooooow." Now it's been painted yellow and other nice colours and has been renovated, but then it looked like something from the movies; it frightened the shit out of us.

There was a chain-link fence around it, and a drive leading to the front door, with all kinds of cars there. Even though Mount Cashel is on the main road, with a steady flow of traffic passing by it all day long, it's off to itself. To make matters worse, as it was winter, there were big snow drifts all around it everywhere and the snow was blowing.

We looked up. It seemed to take forever to reach the top window of the building, and there were kids looking out through the window. It gave me a real cold, wild feeling. I could see other kids coming up to the car to check us out. It seemed like everyone was staring at us. We were afraid, almost, even to go in.

"This is going to be your home from now on."

We each took our suitcase in our hand—everything we owned in the world was in those little brown suitcases—and walked up the steps and in through the big glass and steel doors into the waiting area. I remember seeing kids in the waiting area, and I could hear kids going up and down the hall. We were told to wait outside the office. There were no chairs to sit on while you were waiting, so we just stood there.

After a while, one of the Brothers, Brother Kenny I think, came out and pointed at each of us and said, "You go with this boy and you go with that boy," assigning us to dorms. I was going to St. Pius' dorm and Ronnie was going into...I think it was St. Stan's or St. Joe's dorm. I remember there was also St. Al's, but I think he was in St. Stan's.

These two young fellows came down and it was then that I realized that Ronnie and I were going to be separated. He never went anywhere without me, and from the time we were tiny kids we had always slept in the same bed. I kept Ronnie warm when he was cold and things like that. But that day I felt something snap. It was like a knife severing us.

As I went upstairs, I could see Ronnie looking at me. I could tell he was afraid of what was about to happen, but was trying not to let on, in case the other kids teased him or called him a crybaby; he was only a little tiny fellow. I went into St. Pius' dorm and didn't see Ronnie anymore until that evening at supper.

The guy who escorted me said, "This is your dorm," and left me there. It was as if I had leprosy. Nobody wanted to be the odd guy out by being the first one to speak to me. There were bunk beds down the right- and left-hand sides of the dorm. I was told to pick the one I wanted. You could see who had which bunk because the bed was made up and there was a pillow there. Several had no blankets, but when you're the new guy in the dorm, you don't have much to choose from. I picked a top bunk and had to go up a little ladder to put my stuff on the bed.

It had an old wad-type mattress with white and blue stripes. It looked fine until I sat on it. The springs and hooks were all broken and coming up through the mattress. I had to make the best of it, though, until somebody moved out. Then I would get a chance at their bed.

I got a coat hanger and put it through the springs, and hauled them together so I wouldn't fall down through. Somebody brought in a top and bottom sheet, a red wool blanket—the real itchy type—and a pillow, and I made my bed. I think even in St. Pius there were a couple of bed wetters. The building was heated by old pipe steam radiators so you could smell the urine throughout the dorm.

I was told there was a locker to put my stuff in, which was right underneath my bunk—a set of two little wooden lockers, the drawers missing, the shelves gone, the door hanging by one hinge. I got to work and put the door back on. Nobody offered to help me. One guy came along and said, "You'd better get a lock," and walked away. That was the extent of the conversation. He didn't want to be the first to be friendly. I couldn't get a lock that day, but I managed to put all my things, everything I owned, in the locker.

Somebody came down over the stairs and said that "Dereck" just punched the new guy. The only new guys were me and Ronnie, so I knew it must have been him. One of the other kids in his dorm, named Dereck, had picked a fight with him. I remember charging through the dorm, and I'm sure there was steam coming out of my mouth. I said, "He's dead. He's as dead as dead could be," and kept pounding my fists. The guys teased me about that for a long time after, coming up to me and saying, "O'Brien, you're dead."

I went after him even though he was smaller than me, and I told him to keep his hands off Ronnie or I'd have to kick the living shit out of him and that I didn't care how big or small he was. And, of course, he, in turn, told his older brother, and his brother came after me. He wasn't going to have a guy in the lower dorm picking on somebody belonging to him.

That day I had to prove that nobody was going to shit on us anymore. Not only did I have to pick up for Ronnie, but I had to prove that I was not afraid of anybody. The guy who had picked the fight was older and bigger than me and he gave me a shit-knocking, punching me like I had never been punched before; it was from then on that I knew living in Mount Cashel wasn't going to be any picnic. He showed me that first day that you had better learn to pick up for yourself if you were going to start picking on other people. I didn't want to start anything, but I didn't want to give them the impression the first day in there that I was going to be a pushover. Every day proved to be a battle for survival at Mount Cashel. It took faith and nerve, but I never backed away from anybody. Still, my face hit the cold floor many times.

After that first scrap had blown over, I heard this bell ringing, ka-clink, ka-clink, ka-clink. I turned to one of the guys and said, "Jesus, what was that?" I thought it might have been the fire bell.

"It's time for wash up."

"Wash up? What's wash up?"

It was 5:15 p.m. and I'll never forget it. Everybody took their towels over their shoulders, went to the sinks—there were ten or a dozen sinks down one side of the washroom—washed their hands, dried them off in the towel and brought their towels back. Everybody came outside, walked down the hallway and down over the stairs. I just followed along with the rest of the boys. It was just like you'd see in prison.

Then another bell went off and I said, "Holy Jesus, what's going on?" One of the boys said, "That's the supper bell." So I went with the other boys down over the stairs to the main floor. Everybody stopped and lined up, and again I wondered what was going on. There was a Brother at the door of the dining room, which was down six more steps, and each boy walked past him with his hands held out. The Brother looked at each boy's hands, turned them over and then pointed for him to go in. He did this to every single guy going into the dining room. When I think about it now, it was a lot like dominos falling down.

This inspection was done every day for every meal while I was there. If our hands weren't satisfactory, the Brother would hit us on the head or swear on us. One particular Brother would give a really cold stare and crunch his teeth. If he crunched his teeth we knew we were in trouble!

That first night I was there, I went down and hauled out a chair to sit with Ronnie. I was told to "get the hell up there, this is not your dorm," and I was driven away from the table. I tried to argue but Ronnie had to eat with his group and I had to eat with my dorm group—we were always kept separate.

We all stood with our hands on our chairs while the Brother said Grace. After Grace, we pulled out our chairs and sat down, waiting for the Brother to point to one boy from each table to go and get the tea. Tea was served with every meal. We couldn't have coffee, and we rarely got juice. Every now and then we might get Tang. We never did have fresh milk; if any milk was served, it was powdered.

The tea was steeped in a great big pot with milk and sugar thrown in and then served to each table in old, bent-up, pulverized aluminum jugs. If a boy liked sugar, fine. But if any of us wanted extra sugar or milk, we had no choice. You got the tea and that was it! Often it had been mixed up well in advance of the meal so by the time it was ready to drink it was ice cold.

Each table had a square, clear plastic butter container with butter in it. There was no salt or pepper, sugar or milk. When we went to pick up our food, we also picked up our plates and silverware. The plastic plates were a lime-bluish green colour, with cuts and scrape marks—cut to pieces—and with yellowish centres.

Tables were then signalled individually to go and get their meal. One meal, one choice, nothing else! I'd pass in my plate to the guy serving behind the line. If I had done something to him or somebody related to him, or if he was upset with me for any reason at all, he'd just put a little bit of food on my plate. What could I do? Nothing. However, if I was in cahoots with the guy serving—each dorm took turns—he'd give me an extra piece of roast beef for supper and then I'd give him an extra egg if I was on breakfast duty. That was the game plan. I treated this guy nice because I knew the next morning he'd be serving me.

If we wanted seconds, we had to raise our hand and wait for the Brother to point so that we could go back up. If you waved your hand, you might as well forget it. He wouldn't look your way at all.

There was never any ordinary conversation, although we did speak very quietly in our own little circle. It was very subdued, an institution, like a reform school. It was like something you'd read about in Dickens. That's what it was like inside that place.

While we were eating our meals, we could smell what they were having in the monastery. None of the Brothers, not even the one on duty, ate with us. They weren't going to eat that stuff! We might be eating canned beans, but we could smell pork chops.

At the end of the meal, when the Brother decided everyone was finished, we brought our dishes back. Certain dorms were assigned to clean the tables, wash the dishes and pots and pans, clean all the counters and the floor and put everything away. The rest of us went back to our dorms and watched TV for a half hour. Each dorm had a separate rec room, too. St. Pat's dorm, where the older boys lived, allowed smoking in their rec room, but smoking was not permitted in our rec room. The older boys also had a pool table, but we weren't allowed to go over and play pool, even though we were just across the hallway. If the Brother in charge of the dorm caught any of us over there, plow! He'd hit us in the back of the head or in the face. This was the norm.

At six o'clock another bell would ring and we would take our books and go down to the study hall for two hours. The bell was kept in the hallway on a window sill across from the trophy case. It was brass and had a black handle, and a Brother would tell one of the boys to ring it. That was the last time it was rung for the day.

Each dorm had a separate study hall which was supervised by a Brother. We went from September through to June, and we sat there at wooden desks, all in a row, without a sound, for two hours. We tried everything we could to get out of it. We'd stick our fingers down our throats, trying to make ourselves sick, but the only chance we had to get away was if we were involved in something else, like cadets.

I remember one Brother who sat at his desk with a set of headphones on, listening to music. We counted off the minutes to eight o'clock, then five after eight, quarter after eight. We couldn't do much except look at him, and wait for him to let us leave

After study hall, we used to get permission to go over to Mount Cashel store on Mount Cashel Road. It was a little convenience store, and the lady who ran the store knew us all by name. We bought smokes there, six cents each (this was the seventies). Sometimes I didn't have enough money and I'd say, "Mrs. Bordeau, I've only got five cents." She'd say, "That's all right, my child," and would give me a cigarette. I always promised to pay her the next time I came over.

We'd hang around the store for a while and then go back to the orphanage. We'd probably watch TV for a while before going to bed. In St. Pius', we had to be in bed by ten o'clock. I remember a radio program called "The Top Ten" which started at ten o'clock. We could listen to it but only if we were in bed. Sometimes several guys would have radios on, but on different stations. I'd try to go to sleep, but wouldn't be able to until all the radios were off.

The Brother in charge of our dorm, Brother Coady, was the only good guy at Mount Cashel as far as I was concerned. He came around to make sure everyone was in bed and that everything was battened down for the night. We didn't have to say any prayers, although the younger boys did. The Brothers in charge of those dorms went around, made the sign of the cross on the boys' foreheads and kissed them on the forehead when they were all tucked in bed.

In the morning, our Brother might have an early class or a hockey practice, so another Brother usually woke us up. Sometimes he'd make a racket by taking a garbage pail and throwing it the length of the dorm. Or he'd come in with a yardstick and hit us on the backside with it. The heat during the night was unbearable—there was a damp heat from the steam radiators—and we'd often have the blankets peeled off us, then whack! Not hitting us because we were late, but just to wake us up.

We'd walk to the main bathroom with our towels, soap and toothbrushes for a wash or a shower, then go back to the dorm to dress. In St. Pius' there were about thirty kids, and every night all our socks were put into a bag to be washed. That was one thing they were very particular about. The night watchman made his rounds and took the bag downstairs to wash the socks. Socks, that's all. Jesus, we were bad! We used to put the sock bag in the middle of the floor. The watchman would come along and make a grab for it. We'd probably have some fishing line tied to the end of it, and when he'd reach for it, someone would pull on the line and move it out of his grasp. We used to drive him crazy. In the morning, the socks would be clean and we'd have to go through the bag to find our own. Often we ended up with someone else's socks. Our clothes, however, were a different matter.

Everyone in the orphanage was given a number. Mine was seventy and Ronnie's was thirteen. Everything I owned was marked—my underwear, my pants, my shirts. It wasn't discreet, either. The number wasn't put on the tail of the white shirt I wore to school. It was high on the back, in black marker, where everyone could see it, in reverse. I was really embarrassed.

After we dressed, we went down to breakfast. Usually this was lumpy porridge, already mixed, with burned pieces in it. One of the Brothers checked to see that our hair was combed and our shirt tails tucked in. If we didn't pass inspection, we were given a whack and sent out to fix ourselved up.

We were not allowed to sleep in on Saturday mornings, unless we had played hockey with some of the Brothers the Friday night. They used to play on the rink at St. Bonaventure's College. Brother Thorne was the sports fanatic among them. When we played hockey with him, he made us play like adults. That was the type of person he was—a mean bastard.

On Sundays, we had to be up seven o'clock in the morning to go to church. The chapel was run by an old Brother who didn't have much contact with us. He had to make sure that everything in the chapel was in place for the priest when he came to say mass. The Brothers had prayers there every morning, but the boys only had to go once a week, unless they were altar boys.

That was basically how it went, day after day. Everyone went through the same motions. Even the younger boys had the same routine, except they followed the Brother who was in charge of their dorm. He was like a shepherd, and the small kids went wherever he went. They didn't have their hands checked by Kenny, like the rest of us, for example. That was done by the Brother upstairs, and they went straight to their table in the dining hall from there.

Until I came to Mount Cashel, I didn't know what an Irish Christian Brother was. I just saw the white collars and assumed they were priests.

I became aware that I wasn't dealing with religous people almost right from the start. When I heard Brothers tell me to get my supper, "you little motherless bastard" or "you little motherless fucker," I couldn't believe it. Religion became meaningless to me. These people, who were supposed to be so devout, and in whose care we had been placed, were calling us bastards and fuckers. Where was the logic?

I went to church because I had to. It didn't mean anything to me. Anyway, the priest was only ever there long enough to say mass. That was the extent of my spiritual upbringing.

I think most of the boys felt the same way I did. I know of only two boys who seemed religiously inclined. One of them was in St. Gabe's when I was there, which was a dorm for older boys. He was Brother Thorne's pet. He had access to the workshop room and all the tools. He had keys to places to which we had no access. Eventually, he became a Christian Brother. For the rest of us, though, religion was just a matter of going through the motions.

I wasn't at the orphanage for very long when things started happening that I had never seen before. I saw Brothers hugging little boys—not in a fatherly way, but in a sexual manner. They touched boys on their behinds and between their legs. Although these occurrences weren't discussed openly, it was common knowledge who was doing what with whom.

When I entered Mount Cashel, some of the boys warned me not to trust Brothers English, Ralph, French and Kenny. I was told to look out for my younger brother and to make sure none of those Brothers became too friendly with him, especially English. Brother English was in charge of the younger dorms. Whenever a young boy came to the orphanage, he became really friendly with the child and from there, the sexual abuse would start. I told Ronnie if anyone touched him between his legs or on the bum, he was to come and tell me about it. I told him this time and time again.

I saw English doing things to boys in places that were off-limits to us, like the stairs in the fire escape. One time, I took a shortcut through the stairs. I was in a hurry and didn't want to go through all the hallways, so I whipped down over them. I heard a noise and looked up to see a young fellow performing oral sex on Brother English.

I was only eleven or twelve, and I hadn't even been out with a girl at that point. But as far as I was concerned, these men were like priests. They weren't supposed to have sex with anybody, let alone a kid.

These were the kinds of things I had to worry about, because Brother English was in charge of my brother's dorm. It's hardly the type of thing a twelve-year-old should have on his mind. I had been brought up in Catholic foster homes, where I was told that what a priest says or does is gospel, and I assumed it was the same for the Brothers. No one was supposed to question them.

About six months after I arrived, I went to see Roy. He had been placed in the children's orphanage that the United Church ran on Hamilton Avenue in St. John's. I had not seen him for a couple of years. I still don't know why the welfare system separated family members for such long periods of time. I can't see how it would have cost very much to let us visit each other.

Roy was very excited to see me.

"Roy," I said, "are you happy here?"

"Yes," he said.

"Then for Jesus'sake, stay here," I told him.

I was already worried about protecting Ronnie from Brother English, and I was frightened to death that Roy would want to join us. I thought to myself, if Roy comes, I'm finished altogether. I may as well pack it up and go on to the mental hospital. Having to protect two brothers was more than I felt able to take on. We had a good visit, and I was certain that I had convinced Roy that he was better off staying where he was.

About four months later, I was upstairs in my dormitory when one of the boys came up and said, "Your brother is downstairs."

"Tell Ronnie I'll be down in a minute," I said.

"No, it's not Ronnie. His name is...I don't know, but it's not Ronnie."

My heart came up in my throat.

"Oh, Jesus, don't tell me it's Roy."

"That's who it is," he said. "Roy!"

I hoped that what I was hearing wasn't so. I prayed that he had only come for a visit. But when I got downstairs, Roy was standing there with everything he owned in a suitcase and a cardboard box tied with string.

"I'm here to live!" he announced.

As soon as he was settled away in his dormitory, I gave him the same warnings that I had given Ronnie and made him promise to tell me if any of the Brothers touched him. I was mad and upset with him for coming. The orphanage where he had been living was a caring place, and I had hoped he would stay there.

"I wanted to come and live with you and Ronnie," he said.

I then understood that, after being kept apart for so long, he wanted us to be a family again.

Eight

Mount Cashel wasn't a place to show that you were soft, or to display your emotions. The boys were cruel enough, but the Brothers were brutal.

There was a "sports night" held regularly in the gym. On one such evening, we were playing soccer. I was in goal and an easy goal went by me. I felt bad enough as it was, but the Brother in charge had to make sure I knew exactly how stupid I had been. He stood six feet away from me and made me block a ball that he kicked with all his might. It caught me right in my mid-section. You can imagine how much it hurt. When he finished, I walked out of the gym, fighting back tears as he called me names and the boys made fun of me. It was as if the Brothers wanted us to know that they were the bosses, and that they could inflict pain any time that they wanted, knowing that there wasn't a damn thing we could do about it. They had to make us feel that we were less than they were.

One of the Brothers was a sports fanatic. One winter's evening, after the majority of us had already gotten showers and were in bed, he made us get up and dress in our winter clothes, to go out and sweep the snow off the basketball court so he could flood it to make a rink.

That brother was a mean bastard. I saw him turn a fire hose on the pigeons who nested in the eaves of the building. He had no regard for life. There was feathers, nests and eggs going everywhere. He killed for the sake of killing.

He had a dog, too. Queen was known to everyone, we always petted it, but the Brother put the dog on the boys, telling it to "go get 'em." It wouldn't bite, but the little fellows got a fright. Bro' just laughed if the kid went off crying.

Brother Kenny, the superintendent, was the worst. He was the enforcer. We saw him just about every day. Kenny was the one who inspected the boys in the morning before school, and who checked us over before supper. His office was where we went to pick up our mail every day after school. We'd go to his secretary and would see him inside his office. He had a bad leg and often used crutches. I've seen him break those crutches on boys. He punched so hard, he drew blood. Young men who were too afraid to fight back would cry from the beating, and were humiliated in front of the smaller kids. He had complete control over everyone, from the five-year-olds to the twenty-year-olds.

I once heard him ask a boy if he could beat the shit out of him for thirty-six dollars. He took some money out of his pocket, threw it down on the floor and made the boy pick it up and count it.

"How much is there?" Kenny asked.

The boy replied, "Thirty-six dollars, Bro'."

"You let me kick the shit out of you," Kenny said, "for two fucking hours, and you can have that. If you're still standing, you can have the money."

Another time, we were in the gym and he called one of the boys over. He said, "I heard that you called me a bastard."

The boy said, "No, Bro'." Kenny knocked him to the ground.

Three times, he accused the fellow of calling him a bastard, and he hit him each time the boy denied it. Finally, the boy said yes, thinking that that would put an end to it.

Kenny hit him.

"That's for calling me a bastard," he said.

He always spoke like that, calling himself "the meanest bastard" that we would ever see, telling us that he wasn't afraid of anything or anybody. He used to call us "motherless little fuckers" and say that whenever we felt we wanted to fight him, he was ready for us. He would take off his collar and ask if anyone wanted to try to topple the king from his throne.

People from outside Mount Cashel phoned Brother Kenny to see if there was anyone who could come and work in their garden. He would send someone along. One time, I was working in some lady's back garden, where it was very hot. After a while, I became very tired and I went to her back door and told her I was going home. She said I had to stay until everything was done because Brother Kenny said I was there until the job was finished. This is the type of control he had over us.

One beating I received at the hands of Brother Kenny stands out in particular. It was the long May weekend, and several of the boys were going fishing. I was desperate to go, but didn't have any equipment. A buddy of mine suggested that we go to a department store and help ourselves to what we needed. I was game, and so off we went. I left the store completely outfitted! I had a rod, some line, a reel—the works. Everything except hooks, as I discovered when I got back to the dorm. I had to go back to the store the next day to try to get some.

My friend came with me again. We bought a bag of candy and put the hooks in that. This time, we got caught. We were walking around the store when the floorwalker nabbed us and brought us into the office. He asked for our address, and we told him 67 Torbay Road. He said, "Oh Jesus, two more."

He called the orphanage, and Kenny came up to get us. He convinced the manager that he would teach us that stealing was wrong and herded us out of there. He brought us back to his office, and I knew we were in for it. He beat the other boy, who started to cry. Kenny told him that he was a wimp and ordered him to get out of his sight.

Then he said to me, "Hold out your hands."

I held them out, and he told me to roll up my sleeves. I did so, and he brought a thick strap down on my hands with full force. He was rising off his heels in order to come down harder. I was determined not to cry. I said to myself that this was one time I wouldn't give in. This must have infuriated him, because he made me roll my sleeves up as far as they would go and started beating my arms.

Finally, he said, "You think you're tough, do you?" And with that, he punched me in the stomach. I thought I'd die. Everything went black. I saw stars and thought, this is it, I'm going to die. I started to sweat and fell to the floor. Kenny grabbed my hair, pulled me up and smashed me in the face with his fist. He hit me in the nose and split my lip. Blood was pouring everywhere, covering the front of my shirt. I think he figured at that point that he had gone too far. I'm sure he was scared. My arms were already black and blue, and I was bleeding from the blow to my face, so he told me to go upstairs, clean myself up and throw my shirt in the garbage.

Stealing was a common activity for most of us. The clothes we were given were usually out-of-date and yellowed with age. If I wanted boots, I was given a note from the orphanage for fifteen dollars —no more—to get winter boots. Then I would go to the store and hand the slip to the salesperson, which usually resulted in a look that said, "Oh no, not another one." And then I would be given a cheap pair of plastic winter boots. These boots never lasted very long. The soles soon wore out and water seeped into them, but that was something I was used to anyway.

The clothes issued by the orphanage revealed where we came from in one glance. At school, it was easy to tell which boys came from Mount Cashel and which came from private homes. Many boys resorted to stealing as a means of keeping up with the times and their peers. It was a part of everyday living, and very much a business for some of the boys. They would take orders for large clothing items such as jeans, jackets, shirts, boots and anything else, if the asking price was met. What did anyone expect, when we were going to school wearing the clothes they gave us, and which the other kids made fun of, asking, "Why are you wearing your father's shirt?"

Often, we shared what nice clothes we had, but not exactly out of generosity. When one of us got something new, everyone wore it. By the time it got back to the owner, it wasn't fit to wear. I found this out the hard way. When I left my last foster home, I had been given a leather jacket. It was black and very "cool." One day, one of the tough guys at the orphanage asked to borrow it. I was afraid and said Sure. When I got the jacket back, there was a large rip in the arm. When I asked what had happened, he told me to fuck off. I was upset because it was the only nice thing I had. Shortly afterwards, he took it from my locker and I never saw it again. I was told that he had sold it.

There was no opportunity to save money to buy nice things legitimately. I had been saving pennies to buy Christmas gifts one year. One day, when I came home to find my locker door hanging off and all my money gone. I asked a few of the boys if they knew who had done it, but if there was one unbroken rule, it was that no one ever snitched. So I never knew who had stolen my money.

Eventually, I did my own share of stealing. I ordered items from the boys and tried to steal some things myself. It was very scary at first, but after a few times, it got easier.

I also began to steal food from the super-markets, because if I didn't like what was cooked for me at the orphanage, I simply had nothing to eat. The kitchen was off-limits after meals, so when study hall was over, we would get permission to leave the grounds, and a group of us would go to the supermarket and steal things that we never got at the orphanage.

This also turned into a way to make money. Boys asked me to steal blocks of chocolate, boxes of ice cream, strawberry shortcakes and other rarities.

Coming home from school was the best time. A group of us would go into the store, where we broke up into smaller groups. The floorwalkers weren't able to watch all of us at the same time, so we'd fill our coats and walk out.

If anyone got caught, he would say, "Please don't turn me in—I'm from Mount Cashel and I'm all alone. I'm an orphan and I was hungry," and then he would start to cry. Playing on emotions like this sometimes worked. The guy would feel sorry and let the thief go. Then we'd know who the floorwalker was, and could watch for him the next time.

Looking back, I feel bad about stealing. But at the time, it seemed that we were expected to look after ourselves and provide for ourselves. I felt that I did what I had to do, not only to survive, but to keep from going crazy.

The first Christmas I spent at Mount Cashel, I bought presents for everyone in my last foster home. The gifts weren't much, but they were the best that I could do. I sent shampoo, nice soaps, salt and pepper shakers and things like that. I made sure that they were sent in time for Christmas.

Every day when I came home from school, I went to the office and checked for mail. Christmas came and went, and there was no gift, not even a card. I don't know why I expected anything.

Christmas was always the saddest and longest season for me. I thought that when I got older, it would be easier to handle. That was not to be.

Mount Cashel had its traditions. Every year, a cake would appear, donated anonymously. No one ever knew who left it. The Brothers would talk about it as though it were the most important event of the season, but the whole time I was at the orphanage, we were never allowed to eat it. It would go stale and then the Brothers would throw it out.

Every year, a local department store held a Christmas party for Mount Cashel boys. It was held before most of the boys went to relatives or friends for the holidays. There was always a gift for each of us, but it was unwrapped, so there were never any surprises.

There was also a raffle held every Christmas, as a means of raising money to help with expenses. It was a way for the public to feel that they were helping out the orphans. I hated it with a passion. I felt that the Brothers were exploiting people's feelings. It was held downtown in vacant shops. The boys sold tickets inside, along with ex-Mount Cashel boys, and there was always a younger boy outside, ringing a bell. He had to walk back and forth in front of the store for hours on end. After a while, he would start to look really pitiful, which was probably what the Brothers wanted, so that people would come in.

The year that I was designated to go downtown and ring the bell, I pretended that I was sick. I didn't want to beg people to buy raffle tickets out of pity.

Some of the proceeds found their way into the pockets of the boys who were selling tickets. The Brothers never found them out, but had they checked the garbage buckets, they would have seen that they were full of pop tins and chicken snack boxes. I think that the boys were paid two dollars a week for selling tickets—countless hours for two bucks. No wonder they skimmed a bit.

Everyone thought that the money from the raffle was going to the boys, not knowing that we never saw any benefits from it. No money was ever spent on making life at the orphanage more comfortable. Nothing new ever seemed to come out of it. Certainly, nothing was ever spent to replace the rec room furniture, beds or linens.

One year, one of the Brothers asked us to put a portion of our allowances towards a colour television. I don't know where the money went, but no television ever appeared.

People from private homes offered to take boys into their homes for Christmas dinner. We called it rent-an-orphan. I was never very comfortable going into a stranger's home. It was an odd feeling that I really can't explain. While I was at their home, it was okay, but when I came back to my dormitory after supper, I would be all alone again. I would go for a walk in the neighbourhood around the orphanage and look into people's windows, where I could see people being happy and warm. All I wished for was some of that happiness for myself. Back in my dorm, I used to lean on the window sill and look out at all the lights, wishing that something nice would happen to me.

Nine

As rough as life at the orphanage could be, in many ways it was an improvement over what I'd come from. I wasn't stuck in a basement anymore. I could watch television and play in the gym, and I had an allowance. To me, it was a lot more freedom than I was used to. I sometimes went for bus rides, not really going anywhere. For a dime, I could stay on the bus for ages and look out at the world with amazement. One day, a friend went with me to one of the shopping malls. It was the largest one in the city, and it was my first time there. I wasn't used to being around so many people. My friend left me there on my own, and I was terrified, not knowing what to do. I waited by the bus stop, and asked every bus driver that stopped if they were going towards the orphanage. I finally got the right bus. I don't know how I ever forgave my friend for leaving me or managed to joke about it afterwards.

When I first arrived at Mount Cashel, I couldn't believe that there was an indoor pool. It was the first time I had ever seen one. The Brothers sometimes took their dorms swimming. At first I just held on to the side of the pool and splashed my feet, but the rest came to me fairly easily, and I was swimming in no time.

I hadn't been living at Mount Cashel long when I started knocking around with a fellow who was a lifeguard at the orphanage's swimming pool. He was in a Special Education class, which made him a bit of an outcast. He didn't have a lot of friends. All my life, I had taken to people like that; people who didn't fit the norm. He wasn't nuts or anything, just a little slow in school. We became really good friends. If I was going anywhere, I'd sing out to him to let him know, so that he could come along. He asked me if I was interested in working at the pool. I was, because it would release me from some other chores. He also said that it was a good way to meet girls.

On Saturdays, the pool was open to the public. Kids paid a quarter for an hour of swimming, and adults paid fifty cents. It used to get really busy. There were days we had to turn people away, the pool was that crowded. All the kids in the area would come. My wife remembers swimming there when she came to visit St. John's as a child.

During the week, I could go there to be by myself. At the pool, I felt that I was the boss. No one could tell me that I had to leave. After study hall, when the other guys had gone off with their girlfriends or to cadets, I often took my books over to the pool, rolled up my pants and studied with my feet dangling in the water. I also spent a lot of time cleaning and painting the pool. I felt that it was mine. How it looked was a reflection on me.

Some nights the pool was rented to private groups. They paid the rental fee with the understanding that the orphanage provided the lifeguard. I was always volunteering. It gave me a chance to meet people.

Sure enough, I met girls. Being lifeguards gave us an advantage over the other boys who came over to check things out. We were there every week, which allowed us to get to know some of the girls—and, of course, we would see them first! The other fellows would go to all kinds of measures to be around the pool on a Saturday. They'd ask if we needed a hand with the cleaning, and we'd tell them to come back later. The boys would come over to watch the girls while they did our work and we relaxed. It was like Huckleberry Finn. If you want to paint the fence.... Guys who wouldn't go near the pool during the week would fall over themselves trying to work there on the weekend.

This was the only place where we could meet girls and feel like top dogs. We couldn't afford to go anywhere else. We couldn't go to the take-outs or the pool halls, as we only had enough money for the jukebox or a game. We didn't have enough money to buy a girl a soft drink or a plate of fries or anything like that. But at the pool, we felt that we were on our own turf, and we could strut around like peacocks, as if we owned the place. It didn't cost us anything, and if a girl I liked wanted to go for a swim, I could tell her not to bother with paying. In our bathing trunks, there was no way of distinguishing us from the other boys. We were free of the numbered clothes that labelled us the rest of the time.

The girls who went out with Mount Cashel boys always came to the orphanage in groups of three or four. Only certain girls went out with us; never girls from well-to-do families. We never went out with the daughter of a lawyer, or a doctor, or a teacher. Instead, we dated the daughter of a bus driver or a carpenter. And usually he was a bus driver who was on unemployment or a carpenter who drank a little bit. Often, the girl's parents were separated.

There were some girls who came to the orphanage just to swim—that was as far as it went. They didn't date the boys, they said, because they weren't interested, or "My parents told me not to date anyone from here." At the time, I just thought they were stuck-up, but when I think back on it now, it hurts a little.

The girls we did go out with hung around in groups. We rarely went anywhere alone with a girl —we went with other couples. Sometimes we went to the pool. The girls weren't permitted in the dormitories, and I had the keys to the pool area, so our little group usually met there to go for a swim or just to hang out.

We didn't take many chances on sneaking girls into the main building. Outside, we might try to snuggle into a nook of the wall somewhere, but not inside. The Brothers were always on the lookout for this sort of behaviour, or at least their pets were. If one of the boys snuck off to the fire escape with a girl, before he could get a hand inside her blouse, a Brother would be there. So we didn't push it. Besides, we wanted to show our girlfriends off. We'd take them somewhere where all the boys would be around, like the gym, so the guys would say, "Look who Dereck's going out with!" We wanted to strut around; and we weren't about to take a chance on having our girlfriends barred from the grounds—which is what happened if a girl was found some place she wasn't supposed to be.

Girls were allowed in the gym on Fridays and Saturdays. A lot of boys would be around, playing hockey or basketball. When a girl walked in, the hockey game stopped, the basketball stopped dribbling. Before that moment, everything had been mad. After a girl walked in, silence. Everyone's eyes would be glued to the door to see which guy would come in behind her. The games would slowly start up again, with everyone trying to play shots next to the girl. Two guys who might have been mortal enemies two seconds before would go up to the girl together and ask if she wanted to take a few shots at the basket.

There was one girl that I dated for a long time. I guess at the time I was in love. We were always together. She lived about four miles away, but every Friday I walked to her house. I was never allowed to come in. I suppose she didn't want her parents to know about me. Maybe she was afraid they would ask where I lived. I never met her family while I was dating her.

We often went for walks or hung out at the mall. When winter came, we went for bus rides, just riding around the city all night. We became friends with the driver on the route that went downtown. Many times, when we were the only people on the bus, he let us ride for free. I used to skim a few dollars from the till at the swimming pool, so every now and then I was able to go to the fried chicken takeout and buy her a snack. I never had enough money for two, so I always told her that I wasn't hungry.

Whenever she came to meet me at the orphanage, I waited for her in "our" spot at the corner of Mount Cashel's property line. It was a little grassy area with a couple of large trees that we sat under in the summertime. Someone would drop her off there. Some nights, she would be there waiting for me to get out of study hall. I would be watching the hands on the clock, waiting for it to strike eight. Then I would rush upstairs to my dorm to get my coat and go outside to see her.

When Christmas came around, I wanted to buy her a special gift. I didn't want to use stolen money from the pool to pay for it, so I managed to save my allowance. I wanted the gift to be something she could have for a long time, something that looked nice. At the time, charm bracelets were very popular, and that's what I had in mind. A friend's sister worked in a jewelry store, and she said she could get me a good deal on one, so I placed the order. It was a silver bracelet with a heart-shaped charm on it.

As Christmas drew closer, I waited for her every night in our spot. The grass was now covered with snow, and the trees were bare. I had lost all interest in working at the pool on weeknights; I just wanted to see her. But then it seemed she stopped coming around. I stood outside for hours, waiting, but she didn't show up. I didn't have her phone number, because she hadn't wanted me to call her house. She always called me. I was still very much in love with her, so I waited nightly for hours and hours, hoping she would come. When I finally had to go back inside, I'd leave messages written in the snow:

Please call me. Love, Dereck.

The phone call never came. It was another sad Christmas. I gave the bracelet to a friend to give to the girl, but I never heard from her after. I never knew if she liked it or not.

It turned out that I had lost her to a boy who picked her up from school in his car. That was something I couldn't compete with. I guess she wanted someone she could bring home to meet her parents; not someone she had to ride around with on a bus.

The pool was open to the public for the first year and a half I was there. Not all of my memories of it are pleasant. I remember one evening, Brother English brought his dorm swimming. I was the lifeguard on duty. He was in charge of one of the younger dorms and was one of the worst when it came to making sexual advances on the boys. It didn't matter to him where he was—the hallways, the dorms or the locker rooms—he knew that he was safe. No one was about to report him. His style was hit and run. He'd grab kids to get a quick feel and then walk off laughing and smiling. He was short and fat, very mousy and easy to scare, but that didn't stop him.

One night when he was swimming in the pool, I saw him touching the boys. Every time a boy would swim by him, he would catch him by his mid-section and grab his private area. I was getting more and more upset. When the swimming session was over, I went about on my usual rounds. I had to make sure the lights were off, test the water and check the locker rooms for stray towels and swimsuits. When I walked into the locker room, I saw English drying off a little boy, paying special attention to his penis—stroking it as if it were a kitten. He saw me and told me that I could leave. I told him that I still had some things to do, and hung around, testing the water. I was afraid to leave that little boy alone with him. When he was finally leaving, I asked to talk to him. I was very upset.

"You're a holy man," I said. "Don't you think what you were doing in there is wrong?"

He said nothing, just smiled and walked away.

On weekends, there was a man who always came to the pool. He was older, but well dressed, and he always had money in his pockets. There was no diving board, so he used to stand up in the water, get the boys to put one foot in his clasped hands and toss them over his head. I noticed that he often pulled the boys close to him. He would squirm around, rubbing himself against them. The kids were having fun diving, so they would ask him to let them up again. I was getting kind of concerned and told one of my buddies.

"I'm not too comfortable with him in the pool," I said, "because he's getting out with a hard-on. I mean, there's only young fellows here. There's no girls. I could understand if there were women going around in bathing suits, but there's only kids. There's something wrong somewhere."

Later, there were rumours circulating that a couple of boys from the orphanage were spending a lot of time with the man and were coming back with a few extra dollars in their pockets. The rest of us just put two and two together. To tell you the truth, it wasn't a big deal. If someone got a new coat out of it, good for him.

The man was friendly with most of the boys. He used to take us for drives in his car.

"You guys want to go for a milkshake?" he would ask.

We piled into his car and went for milkshakes. Later, when we were fourteen or fifteen, he started buying us beer. At that age, if I drank three bottles of beer, I was pissed. I used to ask him to drop me off because I didn't trust him. I remember lots of times, he drove down to the dump, where it was secluded and very dark. Once, I fell asleep in the back seat of his car and woke up there. Fortunately, there was another guy with us, in the front seat. I could hear them talking, but he didn't try anything; not with me, anyway.

The way this fellow operated was like taking a girl on a date: wining and dining her before trying to get intimate. It was the same with him and the boys.

Within the walls of Mount Cashel, it was a different story. The Brothers didn't need to use seduction. They were grown men who punched boys in the stomachs and left them gasping on the floor. They had the power to do whatever they wanted, whether we agreed to it or not.

While I was there, rumours had started circulating outside the orphanage about the Brothers molesting the boys. Word must have gotten back to Kenny, because he called an assembly in the middle of the night and started writing something on the blackboard. He wrote "homo" and said, "Do you think I'm a homo?" We didn't know what was going on. He kept punching the board and gritting his teeth. We were terrified and kept saying, "No, Bro'."

"See that gate out there?" he asked, pointing outside. "That's my gate. Anything inside that gate is mine. Don't go outside that gate and tell stories about me or anybody else."

Kenny always had a boy around. There was always one kid who was favoured. He had the latest in pants, shirts, coats and boots. We didn't think he bought them from his allowance. Nobody picked on him. He could come up and spit in our faces, but we wouldn't touch him. It was as if he had a dome around him. He was untouchable for the simple reason that, as far as we were concerned, he was Kenny's boy.

The Brothers who engaged in that kind of sexual activity were known to have favourites. Those boys were outcasts to the rest of us. We'd nickname them after whatever Brother they were attached to. We tried to steer clear of those Brothers. I'd hear warnings like "If there's a five dollar bill in the corridor and Brother English is behind you, don't bend over to pick it up." "Stay away from Kenny's pockets" was another one. He always had either money or candy in his pockets, and he would get little boys to reach in and dig around for it. Sometimes he'd have a lollipop in his mouth. I'd see him rub the candy over his lips and get the boys to lick it.

For some reason, the pool was closed to the public about a year and a half after I got there. There was no more public swimming on Saturdays. It was cut off completely to the outside, and the only people permitted to use the pool were the Brothers and the boys. It came as a surprise, especially since some of us had just finished a lot of work on the pool. We had drained all the water, cleaned it, put a new rubberized coating on it, and painted new lines. We were never given a reason for the closure.

I remember shellacking the roof over the pool one day shortly before it closed. We had turned off the heat in the pool, but hadn't drained it yet, so it was full of cold water. I had a ladder set up in the water, in order to reach the roof. My buddy got in and pulled the ladder out from under me, as a joke. A gallon of shellac came down over me. What a mess I was in when I hit the water! Every inch of my body was covered. I thought I'd have to shave my head.

In the fall of 1974, I was spending a lot of time with a kid named Johnny Williams. Johnny was a bit of a "case"; not too bright in school and considered difficult by his teachers. He had been misdiagnosed as being mentally retarded, so the Brothers didn't feel that they had to hide anything from him. As a result, Johnny witnessed a lot of what went on at the orphanage. The Brothers and the other boys looked down on him, but to me, he was a friend.

For a while, I went out with Johnny's cousin, Brenda Lundrigan. She had several cousins at the orphanage, and everyone knew her. If Brenda had twenty dollars, she would buy twenty dollars worth of treats to give to the kids. That's the type of person she was. We stayed friends even after we stopped dating.

That fall, Johnny got into a fight with Brother English. He said that he had been defending himself from English's advances, and that English had beaten him badly on the back. The boys were all talking about the beating English had received in return. The Brother was a very weak person, and Johnny had flown into a rage and turned on him after English beat him.

One of the boys saw Johnny's back one night when they were getting undressed for bed and told me that I should see it. When Brenda came to visit that day, I sent one of the boys to ask Johnny to come to the gym area. The three of us went down the hallway, towards the gymnasium, and behind a steel door to another hall where we could talk in private. Then I told her about the beating.

"Johnny, show her what happened," I said.

He was reluctant at first, out of shame or fear, I don't know but he finally agreed. I don't remember if I pulled up the back of his shirt, or if Johnny did himself, but I remember what I saw. There were black bruises all over the lower part of his back. And in the middle, a handprint.

Brenda looked and became very upset. She insisted on going to see Brother English about it. I knew it would be senseless.

"Don't even try," I said.

She was too fired up to leave it at that. "Okay," she said, "we'll do something about it."

The next day, Johnny and I waited for Brenda after school. When she arrived, we made our way to the social services office on Harvey Road. Inside the building, Brenda told a woman that she had something to report. The woman referred us to someone else, and we were shown down the hallway and into an office. A man sat behind the desk. He had on a white shirt, a tie and wore glasses. Brenda told him that Johnny had been beaten by one of the Brothers and that she wanted something done about it. She told him that beatings were routine at Mount Cashel. Johnny showed the man his bruises, but the man remained behind his desk. He told us that he would look into it.

We left, and went back to the orphanage. It was fifteen years before anyone "looked into" that report.

Ten

*I*n 1975, after the pool had closed to the public, I got a job as a night watchman in the monastery. My shifts were on weekends and holidays, when the regular watchman was off-duty. I was paid two dollars a week.

Normally, the monastery was off-limits to the boys. There was a long hallway that led away from the main building, and at the end of the hallway there was a door. It had a window of frosted glass through which it was impossible to see, and printed on a black label, in white letters, was "Monastery." We used to put our ears to the door, trying to hear what went on behind it. The minute we heard anyone coming, we'd take off. If one of the boys had to speak to a Brother, he had to knock and wait outside. We were never, ever, under any circumstances, permitted inside.

When I had the opportunity to go in as a watchman, I understood why. What a spot. The place was unbelievable. Everything was polished.

Everything was shiny. It was spic and span, the way a home should be. When I walked into the television room, I had to sit in one of the chairs because it looked so comfortable. They were big, high-back leather chairs. In our dorm, the rec room had chairs with broken backs and torn covers. They were ripped to shreds, with cotton padding falling out of the corners. Those were our chairs. These were from another world.

As I walked around, I saw cartons upon cartons of cigarettes, bottles upon bottles of booze. When I came across the cigarettes, I remembered an incident that had occurred with Brother Thorne. I had been cleaning one day, and a package of smokes fell out of my pocket. I didn't realize I had dropped it until later, when I reached for the pack. I was upset, because a package of cigarettes was something I could rarely afford, and I had just spent my allowance on this one. Then I saw Brother Thorne, who smoked the same brand, with two packages—one in each pocket.

"Bro'," I said, "I dropped my cigarettes. Did you find them?"

"They're yours, are they?" he responded.

"Yeah, there's only one gone out of the pack. I dropped it when I was cleaning the floor."

"Is your name on them?"

I could sense what was coming. "No, I never wrote my name on them."

"Anything that's on that floor is mine." He kept them.

Remembering that day, I ripped open a carton of cigarettes in the monastery.

"Brother Thorne," I said, "you son of a bitch, your name is not on these." I took about ten packages and gave them to my friends because I had quit smoking.

In the deep freeze, there was tons of food. I grabbed a frozen ice cream bar to bring to Ronnie.

"Eat it all before you go back to sleep," I warned him. He didn't, and woke up with ice cream all over his face. Luckily, he wasn't caught.

I'll never forget all that I saw in the monastery. The beds that the Brothers were sleeping on! They had a big colour television in their sitting room. They had women cleaning up for them and cooking their meals. I couldn't believe it.

Since we came to Mount Cashel, my brothers and I had drifted apart. Roy and I had never spent much time together, and Ronnie and I were never as close as we had been when we were small. However, I still looked out for them.

I remember the time I caught Ronnie smoking. I swung him upside-down by his ankles until his cigarettes fell out of his pocket! I guess I was playing at being a father.

One day at breakfast, I noticed that Ronnie was sitting very still in his chair. It was early in the morning, and everyone else was busy eating breakfast, but Ronnie wasn't moving. I went over to his table, which wasn't allowed. I asked him what was wrong.

One of the boys at his table answered, "English did something to him."

"Jesus Christ!" I said. "Ronnie, tell me what happened."

"No. If I say something, there's going to be trouble." Ronnie spoke very low, and I could tell that he was very, very afraid.

I happened to look at the back of his shirt. I could see red marks on his neck.

"Jesus, Ronnie. What happened?"

One of the other boys spoke up. "English whipped him."

I turned to Ronnie again. Who should come up then but Brother English.

"Get back to your table," he ordered.

"Get the fuck away from me," I told him. I tried to talk to Ronnie.

"What happened here," said English, "doesn't concern you."

"Back off."

English had always been a wimp. He knew I meant business and backed off.

Finally, I was able to find out what had happened. The night before, someone from Ronnie's dorm had gone swimming in Ronnie's trunks without his knowledge. The wet trunks were returned and thrown by Ronnie's bed. When everyone was in bed that night, Brother English came into the dorm and stood by Ronnie's bed.

"Ronnie," he said, "your trunks are on the floor. They're wet. Get up and wring them out."

"Bro'," said Ronnie, "they're not my trunks."

"Yes, they are. They're here by your bed." With that, he put his hand underneath the blankets and jammed it between Ronnie's legs. Ronnie sat straight up in bed, still groggy, not knowing what the hell was going on.

"No, Bro'," he insisted. "They're not."

"They are. Your number is on them."

Ronnie's laundry number was thirteen. Sure enough, when English held up the trunks, they were numbered thirteen. Ronnie was afraid to get out of bed, because he thought that English might try to take him some place where there were no other boys around. He slipped back down under the covers, but English told him to get up. Ronnie jumped up, grabbing the trunks. It was never too clear what happened next, but I gathered that English asked him to do something of a sexual nature. Ronnie refused, and English beat him across the back with a broom handle. He was only eight or nine, and pretty puny. He had four or five big red welts on his back the next day.

After hearing this at the breakfast table, I went over to English. "Is it true what I heard about Ronnie?" I asked.

He asked me what I meant by that.

"Let's step outside the dining hall," I suggested.

There was no other Brother in the dining hall, so when English and I stepped out and shut the door behind us, the place went up. There was no one in there to supervise, so the boys went mad.

"Is it true," I asked, "what Ronnie said you did to him?"

"Oh, that's between me and Ronnie," he replied.

"No fucking way. You're dealing with my brother now. You tell me what the fuck happened."

A word about English: he is very feminine. Everything about him is; his voice, his actions— even his little peach face. He seemed to float rather than walk, gliding across the floors. He was also a very timid person, and when he got nervous, he'd shake his arm and make his watch move up and down. At fifteen, I was taller than him, and stronger. When I questioned him, his arm started shaking, so I knew that I had him where I wanted.

"Is it true?" I demanded.

He didn't say anything. I couldn't hold back any longer. I grabbed him and threw him against the wall. I drew back my fist.

"Look, touch him again and it's your fucking choice: a stretcher or a body bag. I don't give a god damn."

There was a big locker room down the hallway. I got him down there, and bounced him off the pop machine and the lockers.

"I'm going to see Kenny," I told him. "I'm not taking any more of this shit from you. Every fellow that comes in here, you're trying to dick them up the ass." It was all coming out. As long as he stayed away from me and mine I had put up with English in the past. There had been enough for me to worry about. It had made me sick to see what was going on, but I couldn't protect everybody. But touching Ronnie was a different matter, and I was going to do something about it.

"There's fellows sixteen and seventeen years old in here," I said to English, "going around asking other young fellows if they want a blow job because that's what you've been doing. When they come in here, you get a hold of them and turn them into perverts."

With that, I went up over the stairs and met Brother Kenny coming down the hallway. I stopped him.

"Bro', can I see you in your office?"

"I'm not going to my office," he said.

I remember cursing. "Bro', I've got to see you in your office right fucking now."

Kenny must have figured I was pushing to see how far I could get. "All right then. We'll go into the office." He went in and sat down at his desk.

"I want you to keep English away from Ronnie," I said. He didn't appear to care.

I was furious. "I'm after seeing enough in here to make this place crumble if I ever wanted it to," I told him.

Kenny raised an eyebrow, but said nothing.

"Look, if he touches him again, I'm going to the welfare officers, and then I'm going to the cops!"

With that, he sat up in his seat as straight as a whip. "No, no, Dereck. Don't you worry. I'll take care of Brother English. Don't you worry about it."

Ronnie wasn't touched again, not in a sexual way.

In August of 1975, my age group was moved from the regular dorm to the oldest part of the building, St. Gabe's. This dorm had always housed young men in their last year of high school or attending trade school or university. What was different about it was that there was only two boys to a room. It was the closest we had ever come to privacy.

There were two ways to enter St. Gabe's. One was from the dining hall through an underground hallway. The other was an outdoor entrance which was on the end of the building where my room happened to be. The Brother in charge of this dorm also had his room next to the entrance, so he could hear anyone coming in after curfew. When anyone wanted to come in late, without getting caught they used to knock on my window and sneak in through it. However, in order to get in, they had to give me a beer, in the run of a weekend I often received seven or eight bottles.

Mount Cashel boys grew up very fast. When I arrived, I had very short hair, didn't drink and hardly cursed. That all changed. I let my hair grow long. The cursing came easy when the Brothers swore like it was second nature. It was easy to get beer too; being big for my age, I was never asked for identification. A lot of guys came to me and asked me to buy beer for them. I charged them a fee of a couple of bottles for myself. We spent a lot of time drinking behind the mall where there were trees and places to hide. That is, until the parish priest decided one Sunday to preach about all the sin that was being committed by young people behind the mall near the orphanage. We never caused anyone any trouble there, but soon after, the trees were cut down and we couldn't go there anymore.

One night, I got caught drunk. This was before St. Gabe's, when I was still in St. Pius'. The Brother who was normally in charge of my dorm was playing hockey, so another was filling in for him when I got home. He was Brother Coady, who was one of the Brothers I really liked. I came into the rec room and tried to sit down, but totally missed the chair. Brother Coady came over to pick up the chair, and smelled the booze on me.

"You were drinking," he said.

"Yes, Bro'," I admitted, "I had a few beer." I didn't lie to him because I liked him.

He took me from the rec room, brought me to the dorm and put me to bed, saying, "You'll pay for it tomorrow morning." I thought, I'm going to get hammered for this. That's what I thought he meant. But what he had meant, as it turned out, was a hangover. And in that sense, I did pay for it.

I could go to the liquor store and buy hard liquor without any identification. Many times, I slipped a flask into my pocket when no one was looking. When I was drunk, I did things that I wouldn't normally do. I remember one night some of us were out drinking behind a building. There was a night watchman on duty who was a pervert. Every time we walked by the glass door, he would grab himself by the crotch and shake it at us. I was pretty drunk, and when he started to pull his zipper down, I got angry. I punched the glass door and put my fist through it. I wanted to tear the watchman's head off. He took off running. Glass flew everywhere. When I drew back my hand, I saw that blood was dripping from the ends of my fingers. Two fingers on my right hand were cut to the bone. I ran back to Mount Cashel, but was afraid to go inside in such a mess. One of the boys dropped a large white beach towel through his window. I wrapped it around my hand, and it turned flaming red in seconds. I still have the scars today.

After a while, the Brothers caught on to the fact that boys were coming and going through my window in St. Gabe's. The window was nailed shut, and surprise checks were made regularly. That stopped my free beer supply, but booze still wasn't hard to get.

In the spring of 1976, our brief taste of semi-freedom ended. We were all shifted back to the regular dorm. A large piece of board was nailed across the entrance to St. Gabe's. We went back to sharing a room shared with thirty guys. Everyone was very bitter, angry and resentful. We only had a couple of months left at the orphanage, but they uprooted us anyway. By then, we were sort of out of control. Everybody wanted out. After getting a taste of independence, we were being treated like children again. We were breaking all the rules. We just didn't care anymore.

That was the year they decided to give Mount Cashel a face lift, and changed the old dark grey to the yellow and red you can see today. As if it really made any difference.

The boys at the orphanage tended to stick together in the outside world. The majority of people at school didn't want to be seen with someone from Mount Cashel. In the years that I was there, I don't remember having a single friend outside of the orphanage. Kids invited other kids home after school to play a game or watch television. I was never asked. It was as if we were in our own group; as if we were tarred with the same brush.

We didn't associate, for example, with the kids who went to Florida every Easter. People in my class would come back from their holidays all brown, and I'd say, "Where in the Christ did that fellow get so tanned?" And I'd be told that he went to Florida every year. How was I supposed to relate to that? At lunchtime or recess, when kids got out of their desks to socialize, everyone went off in groups. If there were a couple of Mount Cashel boys in a class together, they associated with each other. We didn't mix with the rest of the school.

We were outcasts from the start. In the minds of the regular kids, we were just one step away from reform school. It was as if their parents had told them not to get involved with us. We were considered nothing but trouble. After all if we weren't trouble, what were we doing at the orphanage in the first place? A lot of the boys came from broken homes, where there was just one parent and things got out of control. A lot of parents brought their children to Mount Cashel because they simply couldn't cope. So we had a stigma. We were unmanageable.

Within the group, friendships were iffy. We more or less tolerated each other. But if there was trouble, or if anyone said anything against Mount Cashel, there'd be five guys looking for a fight. We were proud. I don't know why. I think it was part of our teaching. The Brothers told us to be proud of the place. In spite of all that went on there, we still defended its name. We never had very much to begin with, so what we did have, we tried to defend. If a boy was at the pool hall and got into a fight, someone else would run back to the orphanage and return with four or five fellows to help out. Guys would run over half-dressed, with one sneaker on, just to pick up for their buddy.

But inside, it was every boy for himself. There was no real buddy system. If I got into trouble, I didn't have anyone to talk to. Families were kept apart. My brothers and I didn't associate much because they were in the younger dorms and I wasn't allowed to go visit them. The Brothers drove a wedge between family members. There were brothers who went in there together at five years of age who couldn't stand each other by the time they left the orphanage. There was no bonding.

On December 14, 1975, something unexpected happened. It was early Sunday morning and we had just finished breakfast. Brother Kenny came into the dining hall and told several of us that we would be going out. He didn't say where. Myself and about six other boys piled into Kenny's station wagon. I was in the front seat. Kenny explained that we were going to the police station and that they would be asking us some questions.

"Don't say anything about me or Brother English," he said. "Don't mention our names." When he said this he squeezed my hand hard.

I didn't know what was going on and I was starting to worry. Then we pulled into the police station parking lot. Kenny told us to go inside. When I went in, a police officer took us upstairs and brought us into separate rooms. I went into a room with two officers. One was seated at a table upon which there was what appeared to be a tape recorder and a note pad and the other officer stood behind him. They began to ask me questions about Mount Cashel.

I told them that I liked it at the orphanage and that I had had no problems there myself. But I told them that Brother English had tried to touch both my brothers and that he had beaten Ronnie. I mentioned that I had gone to Kenny about it. I went on to describe some of the things I had seen at the orphanage, telling them that it was common to see Brother English with his hand down a small boy's pants. I also told them about Johnny Williams' beating and how we had reported it, but that nothing was ever done about it. I was afraid to say anything against Kenny. One of the officers took notes while I talked, and then I signed them.

When we were finished we went back downstairs, where Brother Kenny was waiting. I was afraid, but one of the police officers had told me to say nothing if anyone asked about what I had said. On the way home, Kenny asked about the interview. I repeated what the officer said and refused to tell him anything.

Later that day, he called me into his office and told me that someone was trying to cause trouble for the orphanage, spreading lies about the Brothers. The meeting was short. I refused to tell him anything. I felt that it was his turn to squirm. He couldn't punch his way out of this one.

The boys didn't talk much about what happened that morning. I think most of us were just holding our breath, thinking, "Finally. Something's going to change."

But, nothing did. If anyone followed up on our statements, we didn't know it.

During the summer months, most boys either went to stay with relatives or went to the camps the Brothers ran in Witless Bay and Roaches Line. I didn't have any relatives to go to, and I didn't want to go to camp, so I got a job in a graveyard, cleaning graves. Brother Kenny got me the job; his family was somehow connected with the business. Two other boys and I had to walk to and from work, a distance of about two miles. Our lunch was one peanut butter sandwich and a tin of pop. That was it for the day. I got sunburned badly, but wasn't even given any ointment for my skin.

When camp started, there was no need for Mount Cashel to have a cook on staff for the few boys who stayed behind, so no cooked meals were provided, including breakfast. I was pretty much on my own when it came to getting meals for myself. One night when I was really hungry, my friend and I decided to see if there was any food in the kitchen. We snuck downstairs, opened the door to the kitchen pantry and found a large tin can. The label had been removed, so we thought we had found a large tin of peaches. We made our way back upstairs, one going ahead to make sure no one was around. We got back to our dorm and hacked the lid off the can. To our surprise, it was lemon pie filling. We dug in anyway.

While I was getting paid, I opened a bank account and started to save a little money for the future. I gave my account book to Kenny's secretary to put in the safe for me, because I was afraid someone would find out I had money and try to steal it.

Brother Kenny charged me for living there in the summer. I didn't know that he wasn't supposed to take money. I paid the secretary twenty-five or thirty dollars a week for my room and board. I didn't ask about it because I didn't want to cause trouble. The other boys who stayed were also charged. It was no different from the foster home in Admiral's Beach, where they took my pay. Now that I think about it, with no meals provided and no cleaning done (I had to wash my own clothes and linens), it was a piss poor deal. In spite of it all, I managed to work all summer, save a little money and buy my own clothes. The government was still paying for my care. Where the room and board money went, I'll never know.

When summer turned to fall, and school started again, I went to the secretary looking for money from my account to buy something. My girlfriend's birthday was coming up, and I wanted to buy her a ring. I had a couple of hundred dollars saved up, and the ring cost thirty dollars, which was a lot of money back then. I told the secretary that I wanted to withdraw that amount. She asked me what it was for, and told me that she wasn't sure it was a good idea spending that much money on a girl. She said that she would have to get back to me about it. I became very upset and told her that it was my money and I could do whatever I pleased with it. She finally gave it to me, and I bought the ring.

Later that year, my girlfriend's graduation plans were being made. It was to be held at a hotel. That meant a tuxedo, taxi and flowers. I felt I could afford it, so I made another request to the secretary. A tuxedo cost thirty-five dollars to rent. I could have worn a suit, but I wanted to look as important as everyone else. I also told her that I wanted money for a pair of earrings that I wanted to give my girl. She said that I was wasting a lot of money, and that this time she would have to check with Brother Kenny. I didn't care what she thought—I wanted to wear a tuxedo and be able to pay for the taxi myself. I wanted to feel that I could spend a few dollars without having to borrow it from someone. She came back and told me that it was all right. Brother Kenny had said I could spend it, but that I was not to come back looking for more.

After renting the tux, I realized that I needed new boots because the ones I had were old and worn out. I remembered what Kenny had said, but I figured I'd try to get some more money anyway. He remembered it also, and wouldn't give me any. I had no one who could buy me boots, and no one to borrow from, so I went to a department store and stole a pair. No one ever asked where the new boots came from, and I never told anyone.

Grade eleven was my last year of school. As bad as Mount Cashel was, I was afraid of what would come after I graduated, because I had no family. I had nowhere to go. I decided that I wanted to go to university. My marks were never good. I could never concentrate on school because it was the furthest thing from my mind. But I did manage to get through my final year. Barely. I had sense enough to realize that grade eleven wasn't going to get me very far. I wanted to be a social worker. I went to Brother Kenny and told him of my plans.

"Look, Brother," I explained. "I have to go to school in the night time and take some courses for upgrading."

My future was in his hands. Boys who attended university or trade school sometimes stayed in residence at the orphanage. I was hoping Kenny would let me stay. But by June, I was getting worried. I hadn't received any of the forms or applications for school. I graduated on the fifteenth. On the eighteenth, I was told that I would have to leave.

I later discovered that the government would have paid for university and my board at Mount Cashel, but that the welfare department had never received any request for support on my behalf. I believe that Kenny held a grudge against me ever since the day I had threatened him with going to the police, after English had touched Ronnie.

The department of social services placed me in a boarding house on Pennywell Road in St. John's. I was sixteen. My brothers stayed behind at Mount Cashel. Ronnie eventually ran away and went back to live in Admiral's Beach. Roy stayed there until his teens.

Eleven

*T*he boarding house was on Pennywell Road and was operated by a man I can only describe as a money-grabbing piece of shit who lived off less fortunate people like myself. The room I had was tiny, and I had to share it with someone else. The bed was small, and the mattress was a lumpy one that I shared with bed bugs.

I also shared the house with a lot of other people and two large German shepherds that would piss and crap all over the place. It smelled and wasn't fit for people to live in, but the welfare department saw it as a fit place to put me. I was sixteen years old, with not a dime in my pocket. Not once did anyone from the department request to see me or ask me if I wanted to go to school and become somebody. The welfare people didn't care about the Mount Cashel kids once they had signed a release form. They had done their jobs—why bother to check on someone who had been a burden on the system all of his life?

The landlord was a drunk. He had signs posted all over the house that said "No Drinking," but he drank all the time. There were liquor bottles all over the place. Two women lived there—one was sleeping with the landlord and the other was pregnant by him. One was very dirty, and judging by the odour that came from her, she didn't take care of herself very well. She prepared the meals, if you could call them meals. All I remember having is minced meat cooked in water and onions and one slice of baker's bread. Breakfast was bologna fried up in the same pan that the evening meal had been cooked in. There was no such thing as lunch. Once meals were over, the fridge was locked with a large padlock, and the boarders weren't allowed to have anything.

I spent most of my time in my room with my thoughts. After living there for a while, I became very depressed. I didn't have any place where I could be alone. Even the bathroom door didn't lock. I couldn't even have a bath in private, because someone always wanted to get in. There was one bathroom for twelve people.

I couldn't stand it anymore, so I went back to social services on Harvey Road and demanded to see someone about the living conditions at this boarding house.

I told the man to whom I was referred about the poor living conditions. I told him that I wanted out, because I was slowly but surely going out of my mind. He said that there was nothing he could do, and that the boarding house was the best he could do for me. I told him that I had been looking at an apartment and that another boarder and myself wanted to try having our own place. The rent would have been covered with the money that the department was paying to the boarding house. I was sure they would agree to it. The answer I got was, "Sorry, arrangements have been made." That was that.

I later got a job at the Janeway Hospital. While working there, I met a girl who said she knew me from somewhere. I didn't remember her at all. She said that she knew me from Casey Street, although I hadn't told anyone at the hospital that I had lived there. She asked me if I was related to a man named Johnny O'Brien. I told her that my father's name had been Jack, and I had a grandfather named Johnny, but that they were both dead. She seemed confused by what I had said, asking if I was sure about that. I said, "Yes, all my family died years ago. That's why I was placed in foster homes."

She then asked me if I remembered my grandfather.

"All I know is that he drank a lot, and he lived with us on Casey Street," I said. At her request, I went on to describe how he looked: very tall, heavy-set, with white hair, and one leg missing. I remembered him using a crutch.

"That man is not dead," she said. "He hangs out downtown in front of one of the clubs. I see him just about every day, and by the sound of it, he hasn't changed much."

I was in a total spin.

The next day, I went downtown to the club where the girl told me I could find my grandfather. Sure enough, there he was. His first reaction was shock. He hugged me and started to cry. I guess I reminded him of his son. He began telling me stories about how he and my father used to hang out together. He took me around to an alley-way, where he showed me a name written on a wall in fading white paint.

"Your father wrote his name there when he was young," he said.

I went over to the wall and touched his name. I felt for the first time that I wasn't alone anymore. It was the first contact I had had with my real family since I was a little boy. I started crying. My grandfather asked me what was wrong, and I told him I was sad because I hardly remembered my father, and would never get the chance to know him, because he was dead.

When my grandfather heard this, he wanted to know who had told me that my father was dead.

"It's a lie," he said. "He's alive and living in Toronto."

This was almost too much for me to handle. In one day, I had been provided with more family than I had known most of my life.

I was like a child set free in a candy store. I wanted to know how to reach my father. My grandfather said to go and see my Aunt Barbara, who had his address and phone number.

It took me a couple of days to get the nerve, but I called Barbara. I explained to her who I was and where I was living. She was very excited to hear from me, and drove straight out with her husband. They took me out for the day, and I met their kids. I felt warm and lonely all at the same time. I realized what I had missed, and what I still longed for.

It was Aunt Barb who told me that my mother was still alive. I didn't know what to think. The woman I had been longing for all those years had been living in the same city as me until I was eleven or twelve. She had had another son and had moved to the United States, where she had given birth to a daughter. I was also told that she had had a set of twins shortly after I went into foster care, and that they had been given up for adoption. I reacted to all this with very mixed feelings. I was shocked to discover that my mother was alive and angry that she had never cared about what had happened to me.

The next day, Aunt Barb came back to the boarding house and told me to gather up my things. She said that I was coming to live with her and her family.

"There's just one problem," I said.

"What's that?" she asked.

"My dog," I told her. I had bought a little dog while living at the boarding house.

That dog died of old age at Aunt Barb's house. She never once asked me when I was going to find a home for it.

The time I spent at my aunt's was very brief. After a lifetime of having been told that all of my family was dead, it was almost unbelievable to be living with a blood relation. Through her, I made contact with other relatives. After all those years, it was a shock, going from no family to aunts and uncles and people I didn't know telling me stories of how they remembered me as a baby. To hear these things was wonderful; it gave me a feeling of belonging somewhere.

Barb told me about my childhood: where I had lived, and how things had been between my mother and father. She told me how much they fought, and how at an early age, my father was drinking and running around with his friends. She said that my parents had been very young when they got married and that was one of the main reasons why they had broken up. I could understand that they hadn't been ready to handle the marriage, but out of it came four baby boys, three of whom survived to be abandoned, beaten and looked down upon—all because a couple of teenagers walked away and never looked back.

Barb got in contact with my father and arranged for me to fly to Toronto to meet him. A month and a half after moving in with her, I was on a plane to see him again.

It was August of 1976 when I walked into the airport and saw him. I knew who he was right away. The meeting wasn't very emotional. He had been drinking. He reached down, picked up my suitcase and walked in front of me as though I had just hired a taxi.

I got a job and a car, and lived with him for a few months. It didn't work out. He lived with his common-law wife and their son, who was about ten years old. There wasn't any love between my father and me. We were strangers. It turned out that he drank very heavily, as did all his friends. I was soon tired of being dragged along and being introduced as his son. In many ways, he treated me like a little boy. I guess he was trying to make up for lost time. I felt very uneasy about it, but never said anything.

I went home to Newfoundland at Christmas time and decided not to go back. My father called shortly after I was due to return to Toronto, wondering why I was late. He said that my job was going to be given to someone else. I told him that I didn't want it and that I wasn't happy living in a house with someone who treated me as though I was his four-year-old son. I thanked him for trying, but told him that I was a grown man and that I wouldn't be coming back.

The last time I saw him was in 1979, when I went back to Toronto for a holiday. Nothing had changed. He was still drinking and had lost his job. With nothing to keep him busy, he drank even more. He died in 1984, a lonely, broken man who drank himself into an early grave. What a wasted life. At forty-six years of age, he had never known his three sons.

In the short time I knew him, I never once heard him say he was sorry for what happened. He just blamed other people.

When I came back from Toronto, Barb suggested that I call my maternal grandmother and ask to live with her for a while. The meeting was very cool. I wasn't very fond of my grandmother, and she didn't take to me. She allowed me to stay, but she always made me feel that I was a burden and a bother.

I eventually fell in love with a girl and moved in with her. Ronnie came to St. John's and took my place at our grandmother's. He didn't like it there any more than I did.

I didn't meet my mother until 1978. She had been living in the United States for years. She had been back for a couple of months, living at my grandmother's place, but I couldn't bring myself to see her. She hadn't contacted me yet, so I figured she wasn't about to. As much as I wanted to, I became sick to my stomach at the thought of it. I asked Ronnie questions about her, because they were staying in the same house. He didn't want to talk about our mother at all. He was very bitter towards her.

I finally decided to go meet her. The night before, I had been dreaming about the meeting. I had visions of this young woman who I pictured from memory coming to me with outstretched arms, saying my name over and over again. I woke up to a sunny morning and phoned my grandmother to tell her that I was coming.

Walking up the steps to her house, I realized that I was about to come face to face with someone I had learned to hate. I wasn't sure how I was going to react. I wasn't going in with great expectations, but I had hopes.

I had told my grandmother that I was coming over to take Ronnie out for the day. I didn't tell her that I was hoping to meet my mother. When I opened the door, Ronnie was waiting for me. In the living room stood a small, young-looking woman, who I guessed was my mother. She never spoke; she just turned away and went back to whatever it was she had been doing. I don't think she knew who I was. My grandmother came out of the kitchen and said the words that I've never forgotten—and won't ever forget:

"Dereck, this is your mother, Marie."

I looked at her for a few seconds and then looked away towards the window. I felt empty inside. She said hi, and just stood there looking at me as if I were a complete stranger. She made no motion towards me; she just walked into the kitchen without saying another word. It was then that I knew my real mother was dead. The woman who had given birth to me, who hadn't seen me in fifteen years, had just walked away for the second time.

A loving reunion never took place, and my dreams of having my mother finally hold me in her arms never materialized. People say that you never miss what you never had, but I sure would have loved for her to have hugged me, and maybe even shed a tear for me, because I cried showers for her.

I had a ring in my pocket and was about to propose to my girlfriend when she broke up with me. I fell apart. I was lonely and hurting very badly, so I turned to drinking and pills. Early childhood memories were surfacing and I fought to keep them buried. It was a difficult time. Finally, I decided that, in spite of what had happened in the past, I had to control my future. The drinking and pill-popping stopped, but I was still very lonely.

Then I got a job at a senior citizens' home, where I met Dale Decker, who was also employed there. It was quite a while before I got enough nerve to ask her out. I didn't think she would accept. To my good fortune, she did. On a Monday, I asked her to go to a movie with me on Friday night. All that week, all I could think about was going out with her. Friday finally rolled around. After the movie, I drove her home and she invited me in. We spent the next few hours talking, getting to know each other. As I was leaving, I kissed her and asked her if she would like to go for a walk with me the next day. She said yes, and I got into my car, feeling like I had never felt before. This was the feeling I'd been looking for all my life.

We both knew we were meant for each other, and on July 9, 1982, we were married. I felt happy at last. I never spoke or even thought about my past in any detail—I didn't want it to spoil my new life.

We now have two beautiful sweet daughters: Sabrina, six, and Brittany, two. They, along with Dale, are my whole reason for living.

One afternoon in the spring of 1989, I received a phone call that was to change my life. Dale and the girls were visiting relatives in another part of the province, and I was home alone. The person on the other end of the line introduced himself as Detective Twyne and said that he was working with the Royal Commission investigating certain reports made to the police in the early 1970s. I told him that I had made one of those reports and would gladly be of help to him in his investigation, but I wondered why, after all those years, people were interested in my police report. I had heard and read about some of the boys I had known from Mount Cashel coming forward in the media to talk about the abuse that had occurred there. But I had no reason to expect that anyone would do anything about it.

That September, I took the stand at the Hughes Inquiry and entered the most emotional and painful phase of my life.

In meetings before I gave my testimony, the Commission lawyers told me what to expect in a very general sense. I really didn't know what I would say when I was called into the hearings. I remembered so little. Then the questions came and with them, my memories. It was like an out-of-body experience. In the hours that I testified, I relived my childhood. There were moments when I felt I wasn't in the Commission room at all, but sitting in the dark on a basement step. Feelings and experiences came rushing back, and I was overwhelmed.

After I finished giving my testimony, my wife told me to prepare myself for angry phone calls. She thought that some people would not believe me and would accuse me of lying. I felt ready to handle it, but when the calls started coming, I wasn't at all prepared for what I heard.

People wanted to know how I ever got through it all without going crazy and wondered how such horrible things could have been done to a child. Others called to share their own stories of abuse. We talked for long periods of time, and I could understand, with every nerve and fibre in my body, what they had been through. Many of those people had turned to drugs and alcohol. There hadn't been anyone around for them to talk to, someone who could begin to understand what was going on inside their heads and who could appreciate the mental anguish they were in.

As soon as I hung up the phone from one call, it would ring again.

The letters started to pour in, some signed with names; more were simply signed, "I understand." There were letters from all over Canada, telling me that testifying was the right thing to do and that I should keep my head high. They said that it was about time the system was stopped in its tracks and made to see what is really happening to the children who are its wards.

I've had phone calls from former classmates, telling me that they never knew what was going on. I told them that it wasn't something I was proud of and that the people I had told hadn't done anything about it. People didn't want to hear such stories, because they didn't know how to deal with them.

One call was from a man who was very upset. He couldn't understand what had happened at all. He began to cry, and his wife, who was on the extension line, began crying also. I'll never forget their tenderness, and how their tears were shed for me. I've had calls from people I'll never meet, who promised to say a prayer for me every night for the rest of their lives. One person told me, "I have a seven-year-old son, and when he goes to bed tonight, I'll give him an extra kiss for the ones you should have been given." Young people called, not really knowing what to say. They stammered and got mixed up, and would finally just say how sorry they were for me.

My mother didn't call.

Shortly after that Christmas, I got a phone call from Mrs. Hanlon. She wanted to know why I had never told her what was troubling me. I told her that I had been afraid she would think I was a bad boy who deserved all that punishment. I hadn't been about to take a chance on losing her.

So many phone calls were calls for help. People called to tell me things that they've never entrusted to another living soul. I heard countless tales of sexual, mental and physical abuse. Many of those victims were wards of the government, like myself.

People wanted to know how I got where I am now; how I survived such a mean and unloving childhood to become the person I am today. My answer is that I think God wanted me to survive so that I could tell others what had happened and prevent other children from going through the same abuse. I'm not a hero—I just have a chance to help children and adults through their own bad times and bad memories. I want to make the best of it.

Epilogue

Now that the Inquiry is over, and the media has new subjects to cover, I have been able to get back to a somewhat normal life. The phone calls have almost stopped. Every now and then, I take out some of the letters and cards I received and read them. I didn't realize how important the whole event was to people, or how much impact it would have on them until I received this correspondence. Whenever the Royal Commission is mentioned, it's a shock to think that I was part of it. I do think I played an important role in bringing the story to light, but equally important was the effect testifying had on me, personally. The pain is a little easier to bear, and the memories that I have aren't so hard to deal with. I now know that I can lean on my family, whereas before, I was afraid of burdening them with the details of my past. In fact, they have been very much a part of my healing.

September 1989 seems like such a long time ago. Since sitting at that table and speaking at the

Commission, I've been able to deal with events that had been locked away for years. I was never able to bring myself to think about them before. However, a lot of my pain has given way to frustration. The Minister of Social Services has since made an announcement that fifty more social workers are to be hired, to help with complaints of child abuse. What a wonderful gesture—just what we need. More of the same people who couldn't do their jobs in the first place. Before long, they will become just another part of the whole screwed-up system, swamped with such heavy caseloads, they won't be able to see straight. They'll learn to tow the line and do whatever they are told by the department: don't rock the boat.

I've met with top officials in the department to try and convince them of alternatives. I've suggested that they hire people who have already been through their system, to act as liaisons between the social workers and the kids. They don't seem to understand that to a child, a suited social worker lugging a brief case is a very intimidating figure. After all, this was the person who placed the abused child in that situation. Victimized children need someone who is approachable and who understands what they're feeling. Someone to listen.

Try telling that to people who—amazingly— are still convinced that they have all the answers to all the questions. I think that the department has to stand back and take a long, hard look at why it's there. And for the sake of the children, who have to depend on the system through no fault of their own, officials have to find the guts to take honest steps towards helping them.

Because, believe me, it's a very scary world to be left alone in.

D. O.B.
April 1991

The O'Brien family at home:
(l-r) Sabrina, Dale, Dereck and Brittany.

Excerpts from some of the many letters received:

27/10/89
Ontario

> ...*My husband and I admire you for the courage you have shown in your testimony at the Mount Cashel inquiry. So many people watched your agony and wept with you. ...Your testimony affected me to the point of tears.... I hope your testimony has released you from the torturous past....*

16/11/89
Quebec

> *The God that I pray to would never want this to happen to you. Man has done this evil thing.*

1989
Newfoundland

> *I'm heartbroken for you, your brothers Ronnie and Roy, and for other kids who suffered and are suffering at the hands of foster "parents" and deviant caretakers like the Brothers. Please remember that you did nothing wrong—the monsters who were supposed to care for you did a lot wrong.*

26/09/89

> *I watched you give testimony today. It literally hurt my heart and soul to hear your very, very sad testimony.... For the child that you were to have been so terribly deprived of love is almost beyond human comprehension....*

1989

> *The short segments on TV last night tore my heart out—your stories of growing up—I wanted to jump into the TV and give you a big hug....*

16/01/90
Ontario

> *If my experience means anything, you will never forget the abuse; don't expect to. It's always there; certain things will jog my memory when I least expect it, and it comes rushing back. But it hurts less and less. That's the great reward for confronting the abuser or going public. It takes courage to do it, but it is worth it a hundred times over. ...Many of us, as I did, marry someone who will carry on the abuse...critical, bad-tempered, selfish, just like my parents. ...My mother is now 86, had a stroke in December, looks so small to me now; when I was little, she seemed to be a giant. The child of an abusing parent grows up to believe that he (she) is thoroughly worthless and unlovable, a nothing, like you said. After all, if your own parents treat one so badly, you can't expect that the rest of the world is going to do any better. ...I saw Mrs. Dinn on TV...denying everything—my mother does too. How the mighty have fallen! Mrs. Dinn facing judgment and publicity, and my mother dependent on my brother and me. Little did either of them think that some day the tables would be turned....*

03/04/91
Ontario

> *I was delighted to hear your voice on Easter Sunday. ...As I opened the Sunday Toronto Star I saw your picture. I felt that I already knew you. Then, those quotes of yours caught my eye. "Nobody believed me. Nobody listened. Nobody cared." ...I went on to read the text...I flinch just remembering what was recounted there. What pain must now have been brought into your life by this present act of courage—pursuing the dark secrets, dragging everything into the light. I salute you, Dereck! ...Your strength and grace under fire will help so many others now and as time goes on. ...Trust doesn't always work out the first time around. Sometimes it takes a few tries and several decades but it is there—for each of us—that love and goodness that doesn't let go!*

Printed in Canada